ATLANTIC CITY THEN & NOW

EDWARD ARTHUR MAUGER

THUNDER BAY
P·R·E·S·S

San Diego, California

Thunder Bay Press
An imprint of the Advantage Publishers Group
10350 Barnes Canyon Road, San Diego, CA 92121
www.thunderbaybooks.com

Produced by Salamander Books,
an imprint of Anova Books Ltd.
10 Southcombe Street, London W14 0RA, UK

"Then and Now" is a registered trademark of Anova Books Ltd.

All notations of errors or omissions should be addressed to Thunder Bay Press,
Editorial Department, at the above address. All other correspondence (author
inquiries, permissions) concerning the content of this book should be addressed
to Salamander Books, 10 Southcombe Street, London W14 0RA, UK.

Library of Congress Cataloging-in-Publication Data

Mauger, Edward Arthur.
   Atlantic City then & now / Edward Arthur Mauger.
      p. cm.
   ISBN-13: 978-1-59223-863-7
   ISBN-10: 1-59223-863-7
   1. Atlantic City (N.J.)--Pictorial works. 2. Atlantic City (N.J.)--History--
Pictorial works. 3. Historic buildings--New Jersey--Atlantic City--Pictorial works.
4. Atlantic City (N.J.)--Buildings, structures, etc.--Pictorial works. I. Title.
II. Title: Atlantic City then and now.
   F144.A8M28 2008
   974.9'85040222--dc22
                              2008005261

1 2 3 4 5 12 11 10 09 08

Printed in China.

ACKNOWLEDGMENTS

Rich in stories and seashore lore, Atlantic City has spawned its own tradition of fine authors. My thanks to
them all for teaching me about the place they love: Alfred M. Heston, Charles E. Funnell, Vicki Gold Levi,
Lee Eisenberg, Nelson Johnson, and William McMahon. Most of the short quotations in the captions can
be found in Funnell's *By the Beautiful Sea*. The format for this book does not allow academic protocol, but
those who enjoy this book would do well to seek out their works. Help with *Atlantic City Then and Now*
came from many sources, particularly ACFPL's Heston Collection and its fine archivist, Heather Halpin. I
am also grateful to Robert E. Ruffolo of Princeton Books, Atlantic City's engineer William Rafferty,
Professor Julianne C. Baird of Rutgers University, and especially Kenneth E. Williams, for taking me inside
his city. Atlantic City's dean of collectors and popular historian, Allen "Boo" Pergament, was the go-to guy
for this book. He is matchless for his careful research, encyclopedic knowledge, and generosity. Thanks to
my silent coauthor. All the accurate bits are his. The rest is mine.

Special thanks to Elaine Shapiro Zamansky, Media Relations Manager, Atlantic City Convention and
Visitors Authority.

PICTURE CREDITS

The publisher wishes to thank the following for kindly supplying the photographs that appear in this book:

"Then" photographs:
Alfred M. Heston Collection, Atlantic City Free Public Library: 6 (main), 10, 20, 28, 30 (inset), 34, 42, 46
(main), 48, 52, 56, 58, 62, 64, 66, 68, 76, 80 (inset), 84, 88, 90, 92, 100 (main), 104, 106, 110, 118, 120,
122, 124 (inset), 126, 130 (inset). Allen M. Pergament: 6 (inset), 16, 22, 24, 26 (inset), 36, 70, 86, 96, 98,
108, 112, 124 (main), 128 (main), 132, 142. Atlantic Heritage Center: 8, 12, 18, 38 (inset), 46 (inset), 50,
72, 74, 80 (main), 94 (inset), 114 (main), 130 (main), 136. Dock's Oyster House: 14. H. Gerald McDonald:
14. Library of Congress, Prints and Photographs Division: 54 [LC-D4-13711], 82 [LC-DIG-det-4a05156],
128 (inset) [LC-DIG-det-4a19469]. Robert E. Ruffolo: 26 (main), 30 (main), 38 (main), 40, 60, 78, 94
(main), 100 (inset), 102, 114 (inset), 134, 138, 140. St. James A.M.E. Church: 116.

"Now" photographs:
All "Now" images were taken by David Watts (© Anova Image Library), except for the following inset
photos: Pinnacle Atlantic City (page 7), Boardwalk Hall (page 25), Tony Catanoso (page 61).

Anova Books is committed to respecting the intellectual property rights of others. We have therefore taken
all reasonable efforts to ensure that the reproduction of all content on these pages is done with the full
consent of copyright owners. If you are aware of any unintentional omissions, please contact the company
directly so that any necessary corrections may be made for future editions.

ATLANTIC CITY
THEN & NOW

INTRODUCTION

Atlantic City's first investor was dragged under protest into the purchase. "Not those swamps and sand dunes—not at any price! What will those islands ever be good for?" Quaker farmer Thomas Budd complained, but to acquire his desired farming tract on the mainland, he was forced to also purchase Absegami Island for four cents an acre. Now worth $400 per square foot, it must be the smartest real estate deal since Manhattan island.

The native Lenape Indians were the Jersey shore's first tourists. They looked forward to a refreshing dip in the surf and the cool breezes at Absegami (which means "Little Sea Water")—a welcome relief from long, hot summer days.

Jeremiah and Judith Leeds were the hardy pioneers who settled on the island in 1783. Living in log cabins, the Leeds clan farmed and raised cattle. Atlantic Avenue traces the cowpath from the inlet to the best grasslands.

It took a visionary from the mainland, Dr. Jonathan Pitney, to put Absecon Island on the map. He realized the prospects for a health resort by the sea and began to press the state capital for a charter to build a railroad from Philadelphia to the shore. At first rebuffed for proposing a "Railroad to Nowhere," Atlantic City's founding father was able to organize the Camden and Atlantic Railroad Company on June 24, 1852.

And it took the indomitable Richard Boyce Osborn to put the map on Absecon Island. At a meeting of the railroad company's board of directors in 1853, Osborne "unrolled a great and well-finished map of the proposed bathing place . . . in large letters of gold, stretching over the waves, the words, ATLANTIC CITY." Osborne also takes credit with naming the streets parallel to the beach after the seas of the world and the cross streets after the thirty-one states of the union.

By July 1, 1854, the first steam locomotive pulled railroad cars packed with 600 investors and guests on the first-ever train ride from Camden to Atlantic City. Many communities can credit the railroads with their development, but no major city owes as much to them as Atlantic City. The railroads were not only the chief source of the resort's economy—tourists—they were also the means for transporting the materials to construct the city by the sea. It was this same industrial world that sent Philadelphians gasping for clean air and Dr. Pitney's "ozone."

Alfred M. Heston, Atlantic City's greatest promoter, put Pitney's vision into print. In 1887 he published the first *Illustrated Hand-Book of Atlantic City, New Jersey*. His annual handbooks, which he filled with flattering photographs of the hotels and the Boardwalk, were distributed by the railroads for over two decades.

Packed carloads of eager tourists would hunch down on benches in open passenger cars for a soot-filled ride on the Camden and Atlantic Railroad to Atlantic City. Once on the beach, they were accosted by entrepreneurs who had moved small wooden sheds onto the sand. For a quarter, visitors could change into a rented "bathing costume" in the portable bathhouses. After frolicking in the surf and sand, they would return to the bathhouse, be handed a bucket of salt water, rinse off, and don regular clothing for the train ride back home to Philadelphia. By 1900 four railroads were competing for tourists, and by 1925, ninety-nine trains a day were arriving in Atlantic City.

In the summer of 1870, the city council paid $5,000 to lay a wooden walkway ten feet wide, in twelve-foot sections, eighteen inches above the sand. It was hauled away and stored during the winter, and relaid the following summer. The first permanent boardwalk was built in January 1884. The official street name, "Boardwalk," was adopted by Atlantic City on August 17, 1896, for its fifth—and present—Boardwalk. Subject to seasonal maintenance and some modern improvements, that Boardwalk has remained as the city's main street for over a century.

Although substantial hotels were already springing up in the city even before the Boardwalk, it is this great wooden street that became the demarcation line for the grandest structures. One of these was the Traymore, a good example of the development that inspired the real estate game. Its life began as a ten-room wooden house in 1879. Twenty years later, there was a three-story Victorian hotel standing in its place—the largest in the city. Two decades after that, the wooden building was gone and a fourteen-story reinforced concrete behemoth was welcoming 1,500 guests. With its Moorish domes and towers and elongated shape, it became one of Atlantic City's iconic structures.

The Boardwalk featured the bathhouses, import stores, thrill rides, and stage shows. Two blocks over were grocery stores, offices, schools, gas stations, clubs, and doctors' offices—the neighborhood fabric of real life. However, not all residents were treated equally. Many of the African Americans, in particular, had to make ends meet performing menial seasonal jobs, "three months to hurry, nine months to worry." They were especially susceptible to unscrupulous city politicians who doled out favors for votes.

Louis "the Commodore" Kuehnle was the first, setting up an informal welfare system to dispense food, clothing, fuel, and medical care in the off-season. In exchange, the beneficiaries were turned into serial voters during elections, ensuring Kuehnle's domination of the city from 1890 to 1910. It took a grand jury investigation under the administration of New Jersey's reform governor Woodrow Wilson to depose Kuehnle. He was succeeded by his chief lieutenant, Enoch "Nucky" Johnson, who became the most powerful and flamboyant political boss in Atlantic City's history. This quick look at the city cannot do justice to the full range of Nucky's exploits, nor those of his more refined successor, state senator Hap Farley. *Boardwalk Empire*, by Nelson Johnson, introduces its comprehensive treatment of this saga with a telling valedictory by Murray Fredericks: "If the people who came to town had wanted Bible readings, we'd have given 'em that. But nobody ever asked for Bible readings. They wanted booze, broads, and gambling, so that's what we gave 'em."

Atlantic City became a war hero, turning its hotels and convention center into one of the most extensive staging areas for U.S. troops during World War II and converting them into hospitals and convalescent centers for the wounded as the war took its toll.

It was downhill from there. A brave attempt to show itself off by hosting the Democratic National Convention in 1964 turned into a national humiliation, as infuriated delegates griped about shoddy accommodations and price gouging by local entrepreneurs.

The effect of casino gambling on Atlantic City is hard to miss in the "Now" portions of this book. The casinos not only dominate the Boardwalk, but the ancillary businesses now fill much of the city's midtown office buildings.

Atlantic City Then and Now leads the reader up the Boardwalk toward the inlet, then turns around for a look at other sites on the way back down. Along the way, the reader can wander off the beaten path for short strolls to Pacific and Atlantic avenues.

For a full century, America had only one iconic city of dreams, one great gambling resort, one national incubator of entertainment, and one famous main street. Despite recent upstarts, Atlantic City—always turned on—is now raising the voltage. The time has come to return to the Boardwalk and give "America's Playground" its due.

This photo holds the classic memory of Atlantic City: its wide beach of silvery sand, its busy Boardwalk, and—of course—the fascinating skyline, from the Shelburne Hotel on the left up to the Traymore Hotel. The stately Shelburne was built in two stages: the eight-story section closest to the Boardwalk in the early 1900s, and the tower section in 1926. The chateau-style Dennis Hotel, with its two wings and center courtyard, is to the right of the Shelburne. Next is the exotic Blenheim, its Moorish dome and minarets setting it apart from its surroundings.

Rising behind the Blenheim is the twenty-floor Claridge. Dominating the right side of the photo is the great Traymore Hotel. This enormous brick-and-concrete double-humped dromedary of a building stands on the site of the original ten-room wooden cottage erected in 1879. A frequent guest of the cottage was "Uncle Al" Harvey, who regaled other guests with stories about his own country estate named for his Irish birthplace, Traymore. Like the city itself, the hotel declined after World War II. On April 27, 1972, it was imploded (see inset).

There is no question that the most dominating figure on the Boardwalk's skyline is Bally's thirty-seven-story residential tower. For a company that had started out as a manufacturer of slot machines, the completion of its 800-room hotel in 1989 marked a dramatic accomplishment in the casino business. Even the contractors who built Bally's were impressed by the quality of the materials: "They want only the best. This island might get washed away, but I tell you this building will still be here." Absecon Island has not washed away, but the casino-dominated skyline is ever shifting. To the right of Bally's is a building that has disappeared since the main photograph was taken. On the evening of October 18, 2007, as the finale to a spectacular fireworks program, with its own coordinated musical accompaniment, the Sands became the first modern casino to be imploded in the city (see inset). The national television audience, as well as the immense crowd toasting its demise, could testify that everything in Atlantic City is still showbiz.

John L. Young transformed his career as a carpenter for amusement rides into ownership of Applegate's Pier, a newspaper, and several hotels. In 1906 he announced that he would spend "a million dollars" to build a new pier opposite Arkansas Avenue. Large fishing nets were lowered off the side of Million Dollar Pier to capture any sea life available, than hauled up and displayed to onlookers. Some of the fish became seafood; others were placed in the pier's aquariums—the first on the East Coast. Famous names played the Hippodrome on the pier—including Lillian Russell, Lily Langtry, Victor Herbert, George Jessel, and Harry Houdini. Presidential candidate Teddy Roosevelt drew a crowd in 1912. In 1932 Ruth Smith and Frank Lovecchio outlasted a hundred other couples in a 145-day dance marathon. The man would soon be known as Frankie Lane. In 1938, George A. Hamid took over the Million Dollar Pier. He jazzed up the entertainment with the big bands—Artie Shaw, Glenn Miller, and Jimmy Dorsey—and introduced a variety of animal acts, including a diving buffalo and a diving elk.

Young's Million Dollar Pier is now in the hands of Caesar's Hotel and Casino, to which it is connected by the overhead walkway shown in the main photograph. With financial assistance from the Casino Reinvestment Development Authority, the pier received a $123 million makeover. Like the original pier, the new one also boasts a grand entrance, albeit one of modern glass. Once inside, shoppers will find three levels of stores and restaurants,

over 300,000 square feet of commercial space. Many are exclusive stores like Gucci, Salvatore Ferragamo, Eleganza and Oggi; but shoppers can also find James' Salt Water Taffy and a jellybean store. The corridors weave through the pier, so that visitors cannot see a full row of shops at a glance. They are drawn further into the pier in search of its delights.

Harry M. Warner dedicated the plush 4,000-seat Warner Theatre on June 19, 1929. Strategically placed near the entrance to the Million Dollar Pier, it was designed to impress the millions of visitors from around the world who promenaded on the Boardwalk every summer. Although the Depression seriously cut into the number of live-theater aficionados in Atlantic City, it resulted in a boom for the less-expensive movie tickets. Stars like Bob Hope, Esther Williams, and Betty Grable visited the city to promote their latest films. Studio screen tests were included as part of the prize for winners of the Miss America contest. Atlantic City was a natural setting for the early years of the film industry. Thomas Edison, inventor of the movie camera, frequently brought his equipment to the shore. Among the movies set in the city were Mae West's *Diamond Lil*, Spencer Tracy's *Salt Water*, and Humphrey Bogart's *Saturday's Children*. This photo was taken in 1945.

During World War II, when Convention Hall was commandeered by the armed forces as a training center, the Warner Theatre hosted the Miss America contest. After the war, the theater gradually lost its allure. Luckily, when the Wild Wild West Casino was erected, the original terra-cotta facade of the Warner Theatre was preserved and incorporated into the building's Boardwalk front. The days of Atlantic City's great movie houses are over. Except for an IMAX theater at the Tropicana, the movie theaters are located on the mainland. Although movies are not in Atlantic City, Atlantic City is still in the movies and on television. That celebrated 1980 film noir *Atlantic City*, featuring Burt Lancaster and Susan Sarandon, was a Cannes Film Festival favorite. *Duane Hopwood, The Sopranos, Ocean's Eleven, Law and Order: Criminal Intent*, and *The King of Marvin Gardens* (with Jack Nicholson) have brought Atlantic City to the screens, big and small.

A political refugee from Prussia, Alois Schaufler arrived in Atlantic City via Philadelphia, and eventually established his hotel, restaurant, and beer garden across from the railroad station at North Carolina Avenue. His gardens hosted open-air concerts in the 1880s. Each time a fresh barrel of beer was tapped, Schaufler's rang a large bell and offered a fresh glass for five cents. Train conductors walked over to give the last call into the barroom, warning that the train to Philadelphia was about to depart.

The modern redbrick Atlantic County Court Building stands in Schaufler's place. This is a sober structure, with courtrooms and the Atlantic County Bar Association office on the top floor. The building also holds the county's finance offices and the Sheriff's Department, perhaps affording a degree of vigilance that was sorely lacking in the era of Atlantic City's political bosses. There is also a public law library in the building, popular with both the lawyers and the amateurs searching their own cases. The posted rules would have bemused Schaufler's guests: no loud talking or singing; no smoking; no gambling or card playing; no sleeping; no alcoholic beverages; no consumption of food; do not accost or pester attorneys in order to receive free advice. Schaufler's not only tolerated but probably encouraged these activities. In fact, the hotel recommended one last draft of beer as a nightcap to bring on a good, deep sleep. Even pestering the attorneys may have been encouraged.

By 1925, ninety-nine trains a day were arriving in Atlantic City. This sandy spit of land may have been carved by the stormy Atlantic, but the great resort superimposed on its dunes was an incremental creation by the railroad companies. On July 1, 1854, the first 600 tourists traveled by rail to Atlantic City from Philadelphia. Actually, they embarked in Camden and stopped at the marshlands near Absecon Island, where they were rowed across to Atlantic City. No bridge had yet been built to connect the new city to the mainland. The Camden-Atlantic Railroad monopolized rail travel to the resort until a competing line opened for business in July 1877. Its new terminal at Arkansas and Pacific avenues was fabricated from sections of a station erected for Philadelphia's 1876 Centennial Exhibition. After the fair closed, the building was disassembled and carted to Atlantic City. This terminal (seen here in 1910) for the Philadelphia and Reading Company would eventually become the Reading Railroad of Monopoly fame.

The Atlantic City block originally designated for the wheels of the Reading Railroad is now called "the Walk," a three-block cluster of a hundred discount name-brand stores. Footwear shops for Nike, Rockport, and Converse occupy the spot once dominated by the great terminal. The Children's Place is on the corner of Atlantic and Arkansas avenues, connected to stores that sell sportswear, cosmetics, Corningware, and sunglasses. This booming shopping area may be designed for pedestrians, but it is also a hub encircled by Atlantic City's transportation centers. Arkansas Avenue is the main access to the Atlantic City Expressway. Two blocks north on Atlantic Avenue is the Ohio Avenue bus station. Continue one block northwest of the Walk to reach the new train station. If all else fails for the footsore, those ubiquitous jitneys are zipping in and out of the Walk all day long like hungry hamsters.

Pacific Avenue near Missouri was an intersection with interesting possibilities in any direction. Turn right and head one block to the Boardwalk at the Million Dollar Pier. When John L. Young first built his pier in 1906, critics thought he was foolish to invest a million dollars in a pier so far south in the city, while most of the visitors clustered closer to the Steel Pier. By the 1920s, however, crowd patterns had shifted to the south. Head north and one would find the rooming houses, which offered a summer stay without the high rates of the ocean-view hotels, a useful alternative during hard times. A turn to the left would take the visitor toward the great Reading Railroad terminal. However, the proliferation of the horseless carriage had begun to turn Atlantic City into a driving destination.

This flamboyant entrance to Caesar's Palace Casino is at Pacific Avenue near Missouri. Guests are greeted by faux statues of the Roman senate and outsized figures of chariot horses. Perhaps this illusionary scene should give the gamblers pause. Many of the new, grand casinos on the Boardwalk have built their most dramatic entrances on Pacific Avenue, in contrast to the grand hotels of previous eras that faced the Boardwalk. They present an impressive and inviting vista to the hundreds of "gambler's express" tour buses and many thousands of automobiles that ease their way to the huge parking garages erected on Pacific Avenue.

Although Henry Disston was a wealthy sawmill owner and builder, this elaborate Victorian villa was apparently built without his knowledge. His wife presented it as a surprise gift to her husband in 1872. It was Disston's lumberyard that supplied the wood for Atlantic City's second Boardwalk. The 400 feet of open land, which stretched from the villa to the beach, were turned over to the city and reserved in perpetuity as parkland. In December 1930, the twenty-floor Claridge Hotel was built on the spot once occupied by the Disston villa. Among its frequent guests were Alfred Vanderbilt, Frank Sinatra, Bob Hope, and Princess Grace. Its front yard, which stretched to the Boardwalk, was destined to become the most exclusive piece of property in Atlantic City. The Claridge's famous front yard, Brighton Park, was bordered by an even more renowned street, Park Place. The Fountain of Light that graces the center of the park was dedicated in 1929 by General Electric to celebrate the seventy-fifth anniversary of Atlantic City and the fiftieth anniversary of Edison's invention of the light bulb.

In 1981, the Claridge was purchased with the intention of converting it into a casino hotel. It became one of the fortunate few among Atlantic City's great hotels to be preserved and converted to casino hotels. Most of the hotels, at the urging of the New Jersey governor, were replaced with brand-new casino buildings. Bally's bought the building in 2003 and incorporated the Claridge as a wing of its own large Atlantic City casino. It stands as a reminder of the earlier era of elegant hotels. That famous side street, Park Place, still runs alongside Brighton Park, from the Boardwalk to the left side of the Claridge Hotel. Although the building is dwarfed by Bally's sleek new forty-nine-floor hotel tower, the graceful iconic lantern atop the Claridge is a welcome sight along the Boardwalk.

The first major hotel in the world of reinforced concrete was constructed in 1906 under the personal supervision of Thomas Edison, the inventor of the process. It was also the first to feature private bathrooms in each suite. The hotel was brand new when this photo was taken in 1906. The Blenheim was connected across Ohio Avenue by an enclosed walkway to the staid Queen Anne–style Marlborough Hotel, which had been built four years earlier. The owner of this complex, Josiah White, named his adjoining structures in honor of the Duke of Marlborough's English estates, the Marlborough-Blenheim. It was apparently the elegant afternoon high tea at the Blenheim that inspired the song "Tea for Two."

When Reese Palley first purchased the Marlborough-Blenheim in 1977 to establish a casino, he tried to save the Blenheim while razing the Marlborough portion. He even had the Blenheim placed on the National Register of Historic Buildings. After Bally's purchased a controlling interest in the property, the company quickly had both buildings demolished. The main Boardwalk entrance to Bally's enormous casino is located close to the spot vacated by the Blenheim. The top of its thirty-seven-story, 750-room hotel tower, completed in 1989, can be seen in the modern photo. Both the Wild Wild West Casino to its left and the Claridge Tower to its right are now part of this resort casino. With 80,000 square feet of gaming space, it is practically a city within a city. Harrah's Entertainment purchased Bally's in 2005.

In 1860, William Dennis, a schoolteacher from Burlington, New Jersey, built a two-room cottage on Pacific Avenue, with 150 feet of frontage along Michigan Avenue to the beach. By the time he sold the property in 1867 for $15,000, he had added twenty more rooms. Joseph Borton, the new owner, continued to enlarge the rooming house. By the time he sold the Dennis in 1900 for $450,000, it was a 250-room hotel. The Buzby family ran the hotel for decades, increasing its presence on the Boardwalk to 550 rooms. Its ornate French Empire–style wings flanked a graceful courtyard, with a legendary dining hall overlooking the sea. While other Atlantic City hotels were converted to barracks and hospitals during World War II, the Dennis was the headquarters for the 4,000 medical personnel who attended the wounded soldiers.

When Bally's Manufacturing Corporation purchased a controlling interest in the Dennis Hotel, it planned to demolish it in favor of a completely new casino. However, it decided to keep costs down and open its casino as soon as possible, so Bally's renovated the Dennis Hotel. Bally's spent $7 million modernizing the interior and reviving the exterior. The Gothic ornaments, which had suffered in the salt air, were all meticulously restored. The Dennis was also treated to a striking multicolored exterior paint job. Unfortunately, people who stroll the Boardwalk are often oblivious to the handsome Dennis Hotel. A two-story set of stores and eateries extends along the Boardwalk, blocking the view of the Dennis. Occasionally, someone ventures into the courtyard through a narrow passageway from the Boardwalk to discover this elegant treasure. The Dennis Hotel can be partially viewed from the beach.

Nearly 500 feet long, with arches spanning 288 feet, Convention Hall was the world's largest unobstructed room when it was finished in 1929. As many as 41,000 spectators could be seated for an event. Dramatizing the scale of the space, the helicopter in the inset photo has taken off for a ride in 1970. Between the arches, there was an inner ceiling clad in acoustic tiles manufactured from compressed sugarcane fiber. The hall boasts the world's largest pipe organ. Virtually every kind of entertainment has taken place there: sports matches, the Ice Capades, rock concerts, a national political convention, and, most famously, sixty-five years of Miss America Pageants. In 1930, Convention Hall hosted one of the world's first indoor football games: Washington and Jefferson College against Lafayette. The teams played on real grass. The hall also hosted the Knute Rockne and Liberty Bowls. During World War II, the army selected Convention Hall as its Atlantic City headquarters for its hundreds of meeting rooms and parking space for 400 vehicles.

Now that Atlantic City has built a new 500,000-square-foot convention center to host trade shows and provide meeting space for major conventions, this original building has been renamed Boardwalk Hall. With $90 million from the State Sports and Exposition Authority and another $72 million from the Casino Reinvestment Development Authority (CRDA), the city launched a comprehensive facelift of Boardwalk Hall—a combination of historic restoration and modernization. Using the latest digital technology, the original lighting system has been redone. The dramatic vaulted ceiling and the enormous stage—one of the world's largest—have also been renovated. New seating and modern heating and cooling systems have been installed. The acoustics, always surprisingly good, have been enhanced. Boardwalk Hall is still a successful and busy venue, hosting everything from basketball tournaments to music concerts. In 2005 and 2006, it was cited as the highest-grossing midsize arena in the world.

This photograph taken circa 1939 shows a newsreel cameraman stationed on the beach near Illinois Avenue (now Martin Luther King Boulevard), looking south at the Miss America contestants. The Blenheim and Dennis hotels can be seen in the background. The inset photo shows the Miss America evening gown competition at Convention Hall. The Miss America Pageant enhanced Atlantic City's claim as *the* great American resort, engaging each state in selecting its representative. During the early years, eighty-year-old Hudson Maxim, draped in a toga, would emerge from the surf as Neptune to hand the Golden Mermaid Trophy to the reigning beauty. It took a while for the Miss America Pageant to settle into a routine. Girls were at first judged on a point system: as many as fifteen points for "construction of the head," and ten each for eyes, expression, torso, legs, arms, hands, and "grace of bearing." Norman Rockwell and Flo Ziegfeld were two of the early judges.

This photo shows Bally's Casino, now on the spot once occupied by the Blenheim. Caesar's Hotel, at Arkansas Avenue and the Boardwalk, rises beyond Bally's. The hotels lining the Boardwalk in the "Then" photo have been supplanted by casinos, and even the beach is different. Today it would be impossible to hold a parade down the same stretch of sand. The grassy dune in the photograph rises near the Boardwalk and arcs 300 feet down to the wide, sandy beach. This berm is the product of a joint effort by the United States Army Corps of Engineers and New Jersey's Beach Replenishment Project. The Atlantic City portion is a completed section of the project that will continue along most of the state's coastline. Newly constructed dune crossovers and handicap access ramps run from the Boardwalk to the beach at frequent intervals.

During the first four decades of the twentieth century, Atlantic City, with millions of visitors each summer, was one of the prime spots in America for introducing the latest inventions and consumer products. The Victor Talking Machine Company in Camden, New Jersey, set up shop in this impressive two-story corner building at Indiana Avenue. Often the great opera singers—Caruso, Galli-Curci, and McCormack—would take time out from their recording sessions in Camden to take a train over to Atlantic City and stroll the Boardwalk. Their fans would flock to the Victor Records store. George Eastman's Kodak camera store was also a natural for Atlantic City. At one point, there were more than fifty places on the Boardwalk where couples could have their pictures taken. The city was, in many respects, a kind of seasonal world exhibition, a permanent world's fair. Corporations developed more and more sophisticated ways to grab visitors' attention, from the giant Underwood typewriter—1,728 times larger than a desk model—to a huge Sherwin-Williams paint sign that showed its paint enveloping the earth.

In the 1950s the legendary Needlecraft Shop, one of America's most exclusive ladies' dress shops, occupied the Victor Records corner. It was a must-stop for celebrities like Elizabeth Taylor when they visited Atlantic City. Now diners can enjoy a pleasant alfresco meal at Opa's Bar and Grille, overlooking the ocean and Brighton Park. Carefully restored with assistance from the Casino Reinvestment Development Authority (CRDA), this is almost a textbook example of the best in Boardwalk architecture. The CRDA's design standards call for active facades that invite two-way visual communication between the Boardwalk strollers and the people inside, as well as layering or loggias instead of an abrupt separation between the interior and exterior. They also want varied profiles, a clear distinction between the first and second floors, and ornamentation integrated with the building. It is ironic that this whole block may disappear in the wake of a new megacasino.

Dedicated to Atlantic City residents who had fought in World War I, the "monument in the middle of the street" was planted directly on the intersection of Albany and Ventnor avenues to present a grand entrance to the city. A classic temple to a Greek goddess, the monument's sixteen Doric columns enshrine the voluptuous gilded statue of *Lady Liberty in Distress* (inset) standing in anguish over a fallen soldier. Although draped in togas like the neighboring statue, they are showing none of Liberty's signs of distress. When Atlantic City's first beauty competition began in 1921, it was called the "Inter-City Beauty Contest." It was the featured event in the Atlantic City Fall Pageant, which included tennis and golf tournaments, kite flying, yacht races, and a rolling chair parade. By the second year, fifty-eight contestants showed up. The American beauty pageant was born.

Although the monument makes an impressive entrance to Atlantic City from the Black Horse Pike, most of the distress these days is apparently suffered by frustrated motorists. Several battles have been fought and lost over relocating it from the center of the intersection to a local park. Wallace Barr, former CEO of Caesar's Casino and Hotel, and Curtis Bashaw, former executive director of the New Jersey Casino Reinvestment Development Authority, have teamed up to purchase a tract of Boardwalk frontage from the Hilton Casino Resort nearby. This land lies just to the east of the monument (to the right of the photo). There they expect to build a luxurious boutique casino and hotel. Their plans call for moving the monument back into the public park to make way for a grand entrance to their resort. Those distressed drivers finally have a friend with clout.

When Harry Dougherty opened Dock's Oyster House in 1897, he had one basic ambition: serve the finest seafood available in a clean, comfortable, and friendly atmosphere. His customers would have to dig into their money belts for as much as seventy-five cents to cover the cost of their dinners. Luckily, Atlantic City attracted enough vacationers who could afford a restaurant with such high standards. Harry maintained Dock's for over forty years, surviving the lean years of World War I and the Depression. In 1938, his son Joseph took over. Joseph's wife Anne managed the restaurant when he joined the armed forces during World War II. Upon his return in 1945, they enlarged Dock's. Twenty-five years later, Joseph turned over his restaurant to his son Joseph Jr. With the help of his wife Arleen and two sons, Joseph Jr. took over the business as Atlantic City began to rapidly decline. Demonstrating the same kind of bravado as the city's original investors, he completely remodeled the kitchens and expanded the dining room to 120 seats.

While Arleen Dougherty managed the dining room, her sons Joseph III and Frank did chores, washed dishes, and learned to cook. Once the casinos opened in the late 1970s, the Doughertys again remodeled Dock's Oyster House. In 1997, they were able to celebrate the 100th anniversary of their restaurant, an extraordinary feat in a volatile business. In 2005, Dock's shucked 43,243 oysters. The casinos have multiplied, each of them boasting a half dozen restaurants of their own, many of them with celebrity chefs. Yet Dock's Oyster House remains, a standard-bearer and a tradition that draws both a faithful following and new devotees, although there is nothing left on the menu for seventy-five cents.

Such a simple concoction—cream, sugar, and water—to be shrouded in myth. Legend has it that a candy store at St. James Place and the Boardwalk, only two steps above the beach, got caught in a bad storm in 1883. The next day, shop owner David Bradley was shocked when he opened up to find his stock drenched with seawater. When a boy purchased some candy, Bradley referred to it as "saltwater taffy." Word soon spread about the new Atlantic City candy. Because no one thought to patent the candy and its name, business entrepreneur Joseph Fralinger began to sell saltwater taffy on the Boardwalk in 1889. Sixteen years later, candy maker Enoch James plunged into the taffy business. After setting up an improved manufacturing process, he hired staff to hand out free samples on the Boardwalk at Arkansas Avenue. The story goes that a child exclaimed, "This taffy is cut to fit the mouth." James adopted this phrase as the motto for James' Salt Water Taffy.

James' Salt Water Taffy is still operating in Atlantic City from the same building on the Boardwalk, with a restored facade. Customers may not realize that old rivals, the Fralinger Company and the James Company, are now one taffy-producing corporation. It bills itself as a small family business, insisting on making its candy the old-fashioned way. Perhaps true taffy connoisseurs can tell the difference as they move down the Atlantic City Boardwalk from James' to Fralinger's, although most of their advertised flavors are available at both stores. The James' taffy is supposedly softer and rolled in shorter wrappers, "cut to fit the mouth." Fralinger's is chewier, and in a slightly longer wrap.

William Somers's original Observation Roundabout lasted just one year before a gasoline lamp exploded on June 22, 1892, sending it up in flames. By July 4, he not only built a second one, but he made it a double wheel. Although he lost out to George W. G. Ferris, whose enormous wheel dominated the Chicago World's Fair, Somers constructed a wheel just outside the fairgrounds. It also attracted large crowds, but nothing to match the 1,400 passengers who could ride the Ferris wheel at one time. Somers also built an enormous three-deck merry-go-round near his Observation Roundabout in Atlantic City. There were typical carousel animals on the lowest deck, a roller-skating rink on the second, and a dance floor on the third. His merry-go-round could accommodate up to 1,500 people at one time.

Change is constant in a resort community like Atlantic City. As the seasons come and go, the sands shift and the skyline changes; thousands of Boardwalk shops have changed hands in the past 150 years. This is a typical eclectic row of Boardwalk shops. Some feature collectibles and antiques. Others sell the standard fast foods: funnel cakes, pizza, and cheese steaks. It is remarkable that one of the shops has endured for a full seventy years, a gallery of oriental rugs, fine furniture, jade and ivory carvings, and estate purchases—a reminder of the exotic international treasures once popular on the Atlantic City Boardwalk. Those who prefer the future to the past can visit the Psychic Shop, on the right edge of the photo.

Atlantic City survived its first century relatively intact, thanks in good measure to a fiercely determined fire department. These men took great pride in their work and formed close, spirited communities. Some units even had their own musical ensembles. The elaborate decoration on that first wooden fire station in Chelsea (inset) makes a statement about the élan of the men who banded together for days and nights at a time, and faced the most dangerous of challenges. On December 2, 1896, fire swept through St. Monica's Catholic Church—diagonally across the intersection of Pacific and California avenues from the Chelsea Fire Company. Two of the firemen who rushed into the church with hoses were so intent on saving the building that they did not heed the order to vacate the dangerous structure. The steeple fell in on the burning roof, which collapsed, burying the two men from under the rubble. Their early years, recounted by Captain Kemp—a longtime officer in Atlantic City and chronicler of the Fire Department's history—are full of fierce wind-whipped blazes and heroic feats.

Rule number one: If you build your main street out of wood, you'd better have a first-rate fire department. Fires raged on sections of the Boardwalk as early as 1892, many of them taking out whole blocks of hotels and stores. The "modern" fire station, now occupied by Chelsea Fire Company No. 6 at Atlantic and California avenues, may be eighty years old, but it remains as one of the city's several landmark fire company buildings. These exquisitely detailed Italianate brick-and-stone buildings make a statement about the

pride the city takes in its 273 firefighters. The first message that recruits see is the same as ever: Your job entails the risk of death from cave-ins, collapsing walls, becoming trapped in a burning building, even an accident racing to the scene of a fire. Fires in June 2007 destroyed five stores and resulted in smoke damage to the Casino Control Commission's offices in the Arcade Building. According to the fire chief, "The alarm came in at two twenty-six, we were dispatched at two twenty-seven, we were on the scene at two twenty-nine."

The United States Post Office at Illinois and Pacific avenues was brand-new at the time of this photograph. U.S. Postmaster Thomas C. Stewart was in attendance at the dedication on February 22, 1937. Postal service was especially critical to Atlantic City. After all, the flood of postcards ("Having a great time. Wish you were here.") sent from the city every summer was a key segment of Atlantic City's promotional output. One 1910 postcard shows three men and a woman sitting together on the beach, with the caption "Girls Wanted, Atlantic City, N.J." Another shows six women with this invitation: "There are plenty of nice girls here but not enough boys. Why don't you come out and have a good time in Atlantic City, N.J.?" The first Atlantic City post office opened on June 27, 1854, at Massachusetts and Baltic avenues, and the first postmaster was Robert B. Leeds, the mayor's brother. In 1905, the first government-owned post office opened at Pennsylvania and Pacific.

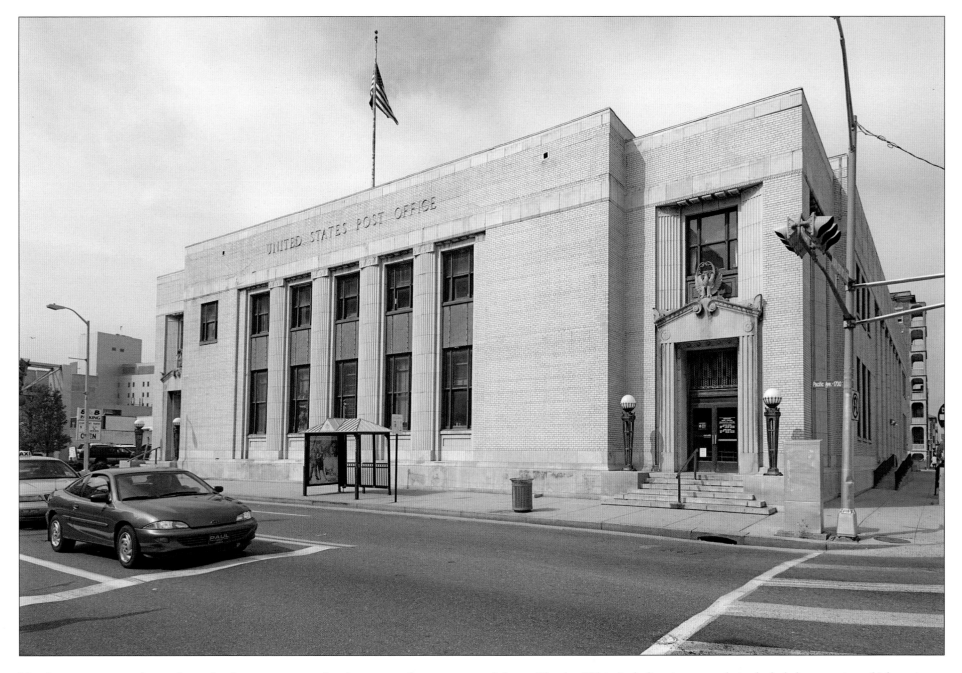

Nearly seventy years later, the only change seems to be the name of the street. The post office is now at Martin Luther King and Pacific avenues. The two great murals, twenty-four feet by ten feet, have graced the building's interior since they were installed during the Great Depression under the Works Progress Administration Artists project. The time capsule remains sealed in the cornerstone—a copper box that contains messages, local newspapers, and other documents from 1936.

Mayor Charles White's dedication speech included the promise of "devotion to that Atlantic City of sixty or seventy years hence when this box may be opened. We shall not forget the lessons of the past." When the new mail distribution center opens on Tennessee Street, and this grand building is demolished, nearly seventy years will have passed. Perhaps the time capsule will be opened to see if the lessons of the past have been learned.

This 1912 photograph of the ivy-covered Atlantic City Public Library shows the city's pride in its new Carnegie-funded facility. The city's first lending library actually began a decade earlier on the third floor of the Old City Hall, with staff provided by the volunteers from the Women's Research Club, the original library organization. The previous year, over 6,000 residents of the city had voted in favor of establishing the library, with only thirty dissenters. The trustees applied to Andrew Carnegie for funds to erect a new library building at the corner of Illinois and Pacific avenues, and received a $60,000 grant. Carnegie later added another $11,000 to his gift. Two thousand people attended the dedication of the handsome new building on January 2, 1905. For eight decades, it served the residents of Atlantic City, as well as tourists who escaped the bright Boardwalk for the shady quiet of the Atlantic City Free Public Library.

Bursting at the seams in this gracious building, the Atlantic City Free Public Library moved to brand-new facilities back on the very corner where it had been founded. Open daily and some evenings, the library is always full. A unique archive of Atlantic City history was also moved to the new quarters. Named for Alfred M. Heston, Atlantic City's first great promoter, this treasure trove contains many of his writings and photographs documenting the early days of the resort city. Heston's publications form the backbone of archive materials ranging from the birth of Atlantic City to the latest casino plans. The Carnegie Library Center, now a branch of the Richard Stockton College of New Jersey, has itself been modernized. It houses the Stockton Institute for Gaming Management, offering a certificate program in collaboration with the Spectrum Gaming Group, a service organization sponsored by the casino industry to enhance the skills of casino staff.

In the early 1940s, as Atlantic City recovered from the Depression, Paul D'Amato was running a makeshift casino in the back room of the Garibaldi Club, a social club for Italian immigrants on Missouri Avenue. The club shared a wall with the 500 Club, which had a door in its back room that opened into the casino. By 1946, Paul "Skinny" D'Amato had taken over the 500 Club and expanded the front showroom to seat 450 people. On July 25, 1946, Dino Crocetti, a young Italian singer who had been crooning in Manhattan dives and Chinese restaurants, took the stage—Dean Martin's first appearance at the 500 Club. The following night, a nineteen-year-old with a routine that involved lip-synching to records jumped onstage and joined Martin in a madcap routine that became an instant sensation. Dean Martin and Jerry Lewis packed in the audiences for three performances a night, including a late show at 4:00 a.m. In 1948, Skinny introduced Martin and Lewis to his friend Frank Sinatra, and the Rat Pack began to form.

No hint of the 500 Club remains on Missouri Avenue, except the addition of its name to the Missouri Avenue sign. On June 10, 1973, the club caught fire and burned to the ground. All that remained was the cement pavement in front, which featured the footprints and handprints of the stars who had performed there, including Nat King Cole, the McGuire sisters, Jimmy Durante, Zsa Zsa Gabor, Alan King, Liberace, Jackie Gleason, Danny Thomas, and Patti

Page. By this time, Atlantic City had reached its lowest point, just a few years before the casinos would move into the city and bring back some of Skinny D'Amato's 500 Club entertainers to their own glitzy new venues. One reminder of showbiz glory still lights up the night at the spot of the 500 Club: the electronic billboard of the Trump Plaza Casino.

This early 1900s photo shows the second city hall building. Completed in 1901, it was roundly criticized by citizens who considered it too plain, "bilious looking," and an "offense to the eye." It was built on the same corner as the first city hall at Atlantic and Tennessee avenues, but it stretched out to occupy additional lots, including the site of an opera house that had burned in the fire of 1893. The first city hall, built in 1875, is pictured in the inset. The Atlantic Avenue rooms served as offices for public officials, with some space rented as stores. There were two rooms in the rear of the building: a meeting room for the city council and a jail. The council purchased a large bell for the tower to ring for emergencies and fires. Unfortunately, one of its first duties was to ring on August 17, 1893, to alert the firemen that city hall itself was in flames. The remains of the bell were melted down to make small bells as souvenirs of the event.

The Atlantic City Free Public Library (ACFPL) is located on the very spot once occupied by city hall. The ACFPL and the Atlantic County Office Building adjacent to it represent a cooperative effort in revitalizing midtown Atlantic City. Not just a repository for books, the library sponsors concerts, plays, computer training, authors' presentations, homework help, film discussions, and a "kids corner." The ACFPL takes a proactive approach to the city residents, printing its newsletter in English and Spanish, and offering a free series of English language sessions. The modern seven-story Atlantic County Office Building is connected to the library by an atrium. The county provides a wide range of public services, including air pollution inspections, aging and disability support, job training, restaurant inspections, children's health, consumer protection, mosquito control, voter registration, and a youth shelter. Atlantic County's facilities include a dozen public parks, the Green Tree Golf Course, nine senior centers, and a veterans' cemetery.

Max E. Blatt was already an active player in Atlantic City's recreational shopping scene, with three stores on the Boardwalk, when he built the city's largest department store. He first opened the nine-story store at South Carolina and Atlantic avenues in 1922, announcing over a million dollars in bonds for sale to fund his venture. Within a few years, the store would need to weather the Great Depression, and did so by holding its prices low. In 1931, boys' corduroy knickers were sold for $1.79 and men's lumber jackets for $1.98. Women's rayon berets cost only nineteen cents. Blatt claimed that hardly a day went by in his first year that some visiting department store man didn't drop by and congratulate him in his "splendid new building." He was so proud of the red Gold-Seal battleship linoleum, which covered every floor, that he participated in an early advertisement for the company. People who grew up in Atlantic City during the 1940s and 1950s can still remember having their high school artwork displayed at Blatt's, and watching Mickey Mouse cartoons in the huge toy department during Christmas shopping season.

By the 1970s, Blatt's was no more; it had become part of
Philadelphia's regional Lit Brothers chain. The exterior of
the building was modernized. Although the basic contours
of the original structure are still evident, its hundreds of
windows have been sealed by a skin of brick cladding.
Only narrow bands of permanently sealed windows,
running vertically up the building, admit light to the
interior. In 1981, the structure was converted to an office
building. The Atlantic City Public School's Board of
Education and Superintendent's Office now occupy the
fifth floor. Boasting a proud tradition of public education,
this central office supervises eleven schools and a modern
high school complex. Many of the other floors are occupied
by staff of the New Jersey Casino Control Commission,
including a special unit of the New Jersey State Police.
This is the only law-enforcement agency permitted to have
officers on the floors of Atlantic City's casinos. The good
old days when the city's youngsters enjoyed Blatt's eye-
popping displays and dreamed of Christmas presents to
come are long gone. Except for the convenience store on
the first floor, there is not much to draw Atlantic City's
students into the building.

Thanks to Jesse S. Lake, Atlantic City boasted two revolving towers on the Boardwalk in 1895: one at Massachusetts Avenue, and this one at New York Avenue. These steel towers were 125 feet tall. As many as forty passengers at one time could pay ten cents apiece to board a circular elevator. It slowly turned as it ascended to a height of 103 feet, then it gradually circled back down to platform level. The Lakes were prolific inventors, earning sixty-five different patents for their devices, including an improved cable-car grip, a process to extract aluminum from tidal marshes, and the Caterpillar tractor. To keep their hay cart from being bogged down in the marshes between Atlantic City and Pleasantville, they installed tractor-style chains on the wheels. Due to the intolerable noise caused by the device, the cart was called "Lake's Hell Wagon."

The thirty-four-floor Atlantic Palace now presides over this section of the Boardwalk, dwarfing everything around it. Fantasea Resorts owns this resort along with the Flagship in the Inlet section—and, across the bay, La Sammana in Brigantine. The view from the upper floors of Atlantic Palace is one of the best in the city. Guests can make standard reservations at this moderately priced hotel, or they can meet with staff to consider time-share options offered by Fantasea Resorts. The beach has widened considerably over the past hundred years. Apparently, the piers have an effect akin to breakers, causing the sea to deposit more sand than it washes away.

Although grand hotels dominated the Boardwalk when this photo was taken in 1932, most of the stores were comparatively modest. The graceful arch of the Boardwalk National Bank was an exception. It housed the only bank with a presence on the Boardwalk, as well as shops like Fralinger's Salt Water Taffy on the Tennessee Avenue corner. Joseph F. Fralinger is immortalized on his boxes of saltwater taffy, but he supported a wide variety of enterprises in Atlantic City. At first he managed a baseball team, and then a cider stand on the Boardwalk, as well as a cigar store. After he became financially successful, he built the Academy of Music at New York Avenue, and a theater and concert hall later named the Apollo Theatre. Opposite Fralinger's, on the other side of the Arcade entrance, is the Porto Rico Store. Visitors to Atlantic City could find a variety of imported wares from Turkey, Armenia, Syria, China, Japan, Mexico, Egypt, India, Italy, and France.

Fralinger's is still selling its saltwater taffy from the corner shop of the Arcade Building, but the rest of the building has different tenants. Most of the building now serves as offices for the New Jersey Casino Control Commission. The Arcade Building extends for nearly half a block toward Pacific Avenue and originally featured a two-story atrium that ran the length of the building. The interior has been substantially modified to accommodate offices for the Casino Control Commission. From the start, the commission has established a reputation for holding the casino operators in Atlantic City to a very high standard. It has been known to deny licenses to casinos if their officers have unsavory reputations, and it has even suspended licenses for established casinos if their operations have faltered. The New Jersey Casino Control Commission takes its mission to "assure the public trust and confidence in the credibility and integrity of the casino operations" very seriously.

Atlantic City's amusement-ride builders experimented with all sorts of coasters. One version of the Switchback consisted of two straight parallel tracks, curving up at the ends. Riders would climb stairs to race along one track, disembark at the end, and clamber up to the other track for a ride back. The *Daily Union* in 1893 related plans for a combination Ferris wheel and roller coaster. A member of the inventive Lake family constructed the popular "Haunted Swing" in 1894. Twenty people would sit in a suspended car that seemed to swing higher and higher until it made a complete loop. The ride was a grand illusion, because it was the actual room—walls, ceiling, and well-secured furniture—that actually revolved, while the swing remained stationary. In 1902, the Loop-the-Loop, or Flip-Flap Railway, was constructed on Young's Pier. Although many of the riders emerged with neck and back injuries because of the jerking motion of the ride, it was the ultimate thrill ride for the most adventurous.

Central Pier, shortened by fire and storm, still has visitors careening around in circles. Now they are riding on a go-kart track—and presumably not making full loops. Most of the pier's technology is now invested in small-scale amusements; Central Pier specializes in arcade games. Families can visit reasonably priced fast-food stands and relax at the picnic tables that dot the pier, affording a pleasant view of the sea, surf, and Boardwalk. The deck of Central Pier is a marked contrast to the Boardwalk itself. Beginning in 1991, the Boardwalk was resurfaced with Brazilian hardwood. Its fine, hard grain offers a smooth surface for strollers, and it is likely to endure the elements for as long as forty years. The pier, however, still has the traditional southern yellow pine, a wood that splinters easily and has a life of only ten years.

Auditorium Pier was constructed in 1899 at the foot of Pennsylvania Avenue amid a flurry of controversy. Major hotels objected that the pier blocked their view. Others complained that new performance space competed with other theaters along the Boardwalk. Only 500 feet long, the pier did not meet Atlantic City's 1,000-foot requirement. Consequently, the city refused to connect the pier to the Boardwalk. George Cornelius Tilyou, who had built the Steeplechase amusement rides at Coney Island, purchased the pier and reopened it as Steeplechase Pier in 1904. He soon added a large Ferris wheel and wild rides like the Whirlpool and the Whip to his "Playground of Innocent Amusement for Young and Old." The Wild Chair ride flung riders out over the ocean. Tilyou installed an enormous clown mouth as the entrance to the pier. In 1926, the world's largest electric sign—the 215-foot-long, 26,000-bulb Chesterfield cigarette billboard—was mounted on the roof of the auditorium, early proof that Atlantic City was "always turned on."

The great sign collapsed in a fire in 1932. Unfortunately, in 1988, a fire gutted Steeplechase Pier. The pier shown here is the Steel Pier: Steeplechase was demolished in 1996. All that remains of Tilyou's great pier, ironically, is the wooden apron built to connect the pier to the Boardwalk. A take-out eatery now occupies that apron. The large freestanding billboard is an unintentional tribute to what was once there. In 1915, the Boardwalk's two-by-fours were laid in the same graceful herringbone pattern still used today. This permitted more even wear as the rolling chairs were pushed up and down. Atlantic City's Office of Engineering and its twenty-eight-person Boardwalk maintenance crew are constantly exploring ways to improve the city's great wooden way. They have even experimented with artificial wood planks. Not only did they prove less fire-resistant than the tight-grained Brazilian wood, they held so much summer heat that they burned right through people's shoes.

The Westside All Wars Memorial Building at Adriatic and Kentucky avenues billed itself as the site for Atlantic City's "most outstanding conventions." The building was dedicated to black soldiers, who were often in segregated units in the World Wars. Built in 1925, it originally included dormitories for returning veterans. African Americans represented one of the first sizable ethnic groups to migrate to Atlantic City in the nineteenth century, many of them from plantations in the South. They did much of the heavy labor needed to build this booming city, and remained to perform many of the service occupations. By 1915, 27 percent of Atlantic City's residential population was African American, and they built a vibrant, self-sufficient community. At the time this photo was taken, African Americans ran ten restaurants, ten hotels, ten medical offices, and twenty-nine beauty parlors—including the Apex News & Hair Company, founded by the "Madame" Sara Spencer Washington.

The plain brick Westside All Wars Memorial Building for black veterans survived, unlike the highly decorated stone All Wars Memorial Building erected for white veterans—originally located at States and Pacific avenues, and demolished in 1997 to allow for a Trump casino. In a state of neglect, the African American memorial was also in danger of demolition. Elbowed as they were to the north side of Atlantic City, African Americans developed a rich community life, with their own social centers, cafés, and clubs.

Unfortunately, the glory days of the cafés—particularly Club Harlem, which boasted America's top entertainers and the best shows between New York and New Orleans—disappeared by the 1980s. Most headliners are now featured on the casinos' stages, like the House of Blues at the Showboat. In 2005 Atlantic City allocated $11.2 million to restore the Westside All Wars Memorial. With two modern additions, the renovated building boasts three ballrooms, up-to-date kitchens, and a memorial to Atlantic City's veterans.

Under Frank P. Gravatt, who managed the Steel Pier from 1925 to 1945, it lived up to its reputation as the "Showplace of the Nation." The Steel Pier was a show business incubator, where many great careers were launched. The stars returned summer after summer: Frank Sinatra, Amos and Andy, the Three Stooges, Ozzie Nelson, Abbott and Costello, Milton Berle, Burns and Allen, the Andrews Sisters, and Henny Youngman. Jules Falk, the Steel Pier's impresario, discovered a young baritone singing in a Philadelphia church and brought him to fill in for a temperamental opera star in Atlantic City; Nelson Eddy would soon become America's great movie musical heartthrob.

All the great live shows have moved across the Boardwalk to the Taj Mahal Casino. Sinatra and the Andrews Sisters have been replaced by Trace Adkins, Keith Urban, and Carrie Underwood. Larry the Cable Guy is filling in for the departed Milton Berle. There is no more vaudeville, but the Halloween party at the Casbah Nightclub may be a good substitute. Besides, in the good old days, tourists did not get to meet Pamela Anderson or "the Donald." The

Steel Pier is still a magical place to be under the night lights. The carousel (inset) is all aglow. Ferris wheel riders can see the lights blazing all along the Boardwalk as they revolve skyward. If they want a closer view of the casino-lit horizon, they can take a helicopter ride, which takes off from the end of the pier. They can compound their thrills on the disco ride, the first of its kind on the East Coast.

From its opening on Saturday, June 18, 1898, the Steel Pier began to create its own legend. At 1,780 feet, six football fields long, it offered an amusement world of delights. The Boardwalk end was originally a two-story open arcade where people on the Steel Pier could people-watch the strollers on the great wooden way. By the time this photo was taken in the 1920s, the front end had been converted into an exhibition hall full of General Motors' latest cars, a practice that lasted more than four decades. People who paid the ten-cent admission to the pier could enjoy an enormous variety of entertainment. "America's Luckiest Fool" in 1930 spent forty-nine days sitting on a thirteen-inch disk at the top of a flagpole. In the dance hall, "gay couples whirl in entrancing waltzes above the rolling waves of the big, broad Atlantic." Besides all the headline entertainment, operas, and animal acts, a children's revue spotlighted youngsters with promising talent—among them, Frankie Avalon and Andrea McArdle.

The days when a million people walked through the entrance to America's most famous pier each summer are no more. Crowds are no longer greeted by the wild women of Borneo, boxing cats, or Rex the Wonder Dog on his skis. Instead, the kiosks in front sell funnel cakes, sausages, and curly fries. But once on the pier, thanks to the Catanoso brothers' adroitly selected amusements, visitors can still enjoy many hours of good times. The two-story building that presides over the entrance to the pier is designed to match the maharaja theme of the Taj Mahal Casino. The overhead walkway that connects the casino to the pier does provide an interesting architectural element. Unfortunately, most of the entrance structure's decoration looks flat and artificial. Casinos are not held to the design guidelines advocated by the Casino Reinvestment Development Authority for the Boardwalk shops; instead of plastic or fiberglass decorations, CRDA encourages "active facades" composed of stone, brick, or terra-cotta.

This photo of the Ingersoll Roller Coaster was taken in 1910. Early roller coasters were comparatively primitive affairs with descriptive names like the Switchback, the Scenic Railway, the Serpentine Railway, and the Casino Toboggan Slide, advertised in 1890 as "the most exhilarating and novel amusement in the country." LaMarcus Adna Thompson's Scenic Railway improved on the Switchback. It featured a curved track, as well as a power hoist to haul the cars up the first hill. The first example of this technology in America was the inclined cog railway used by the Reading Railroad to haul coal cars up Mauch Chunk in northeastern Pennsylvania. By 1870, it too had been converted to an amusement ride.

This striking building was constructed on the site of the Ingersoll Roller Coaster and became home to the Stanley Theatre in 1925. With the exterior restored, the interior has been remodeled to accommodate Lucky Lou's Tattoos. The twists and turns that riders experienced a century ago riding Ingersoll's Roller Coaster on this spot are now marked in miniature. According to Lou's staff, butterflies and roses are popular selections among the thousands of designs. Lucky Lou does a landmark business for tourists, military personnel, and customers seeking to obliterate an earlier tattoo.

Charles Funnell alluded to the "peek-a-boo exoticism" that showed up even in Atlantic City's early tourist materials, postcards full of double entendres and coy descriptions like Heston's "Bevies of girls dressed in dainty costumes are scattered about on the sand." Promoting itself as a family resort, one city official in 1890 insisted: "I would like Atlantic City to be known as a place where mothers could send their daughters; and husbands send their wives without fear." Realistically, in a Victorian era when hardly an ankle showed in public, one of the great lures of the beach resort was just the opposite. Even the city's official seal is disingenuous. Despite the pious Latin banner proclaiming "Counsel and Prudence," it features goddesses in togas sporting decorations that hint at delights to come.

This fall photograph shows a beach devoid of beauties. Of course, in the height of summer, visitors can still find plenty of beauties sunning themselves or cavorting on the beach in their "dainty costumes." The sumptuous interiors of the modern casinos and their exotic revues showcase plenty of beauty. The Steel Pier's companion casino offers stunning beauty in all forms, from its

"$14 million worth of German crystal chandeliers" and its seven carved two-ton elephants to its imported Carrera marble—Michelangelo's marble of choice. The Taj Mahal's Casbah nightclub also advertises the Casbah Dancers. Evidently, Atlantic City's "peek-a-boo exoticism" is alive and well.

The photographer who took this picture must have been standing near the entrance to the Steel Pier. Several blocks north, the intriguing Moorish roofline of the States Avenue Opera House can be seen. This is the fifth and final Boardwalk, virtually brand-new when this photo was taken in 1900. Owners of shops that faced the Boardwalk discovered the popularity of their locations very quickly, and they pressed the city so they could build their entrances as close to the walk as possible. However, as merchants started to build pavilions between the Boardwalk and the ocean, like the ones in the photograph, the city eventually stepped in to stop the practice. The large building that presided at the ocean end of Heinz Pier can be seen through the uprights of the pavilion. Henry J. Heinz of Pittsburgh purchased the most northern of Atlantic City's piers in 1898 and used it to promote his food products. People wore their finery when they promenaded on the Boardwalk. Bathing dress was not permitted.

Honoring Atlantic City's long tradition of hyberbole, Donald Trump's Taj Mahal Casino and Hotel makes the claim that it is the eighth wonder of the world. The *New York Times* observed, "The Taj has enough onion domes and minarets to fill an Indian theme park, and enough mirrors and chandeliers to make Tavern on the Green look undecorated." From the two-ton "stone" elephants to the grand stairway to nowhere, the Taj Mahal is the most exotic building on the Boardwalk. Like the Moorish buildings of Atlantic City's earlier eras, it contributes to the flamboyance of the skyline. *New York Times* writer Paul Goldberger called it "Atlantic City with a booster shot made up of one part Las Vegas and one part Disneyland." The architect, Francis X. Dumont, carried the theme of a maharajah's palace throughout the interior as well. Even the doormen are dressed in turbans and flowing robes.

The last of the great Atlantic City piers to be constructed, the Garden Pier was built at the foot of New Jersey Avenue in 1913. Arcades of shops lining the outer edges of the pier faced a central promenade of flower beds, gazebos, shrubbery, and a small pond. Only 600 feet long, the pier featured a four-story building with castlelike towers on its corners—a combination ballroom, exhibition hall, and theater at the ocean end. The Garden Pier amassed its own list of firsts, including the first Golden Mermaid competition in 1921, forerunner to the Miss America contest. The world premiere of *Tobacco Road* took place in the theater. Rudolph Valentino began his career in the ballroom as a Latin dance instructor. A host of famous entertainers appeared at the Garden Pier—among them Eddie Cantor, Fanny Brice, John Philip Sousa, and Gypsy Rose Lee. Harry Houdini dangled from one of the towers.

Just a few months after Atlantic City took over the Garden Pier, the great hurricane of 1944 wiped out the ocean end of the pier, including the historic theater. Remains of the pier's timbers still protrude above the surf. The city restored the Boardwalk end of the pier, erecting the Art Center on the left and the Atlantic City Historical Museum on the right. The exhibit includes collectibles, old photographs, a Mr. Peanut, and a vintage wicker Boardwalk rolling chair. Overlooking the Garden Pier is an enormous new casino complex being erected across the Boardwalk. Revel Entertainment, backed by Morgan Stanley, is building a $2 billion megaresort between New Jersey and Metropolitan avenues. Its planned twin hotel towers will hold 1,900 rooms. Revel apparently has hopes of purchasing the Garden Pier and restoring its attractions.

The Atlantic City of the late 1800s was a community of wooden houses, picket fences, and shady foliage, where the church steeples were still among the tallest structures in sight. Many of the visitors who commuted by train had only Sunday off from their regular jobs. Once the train deposited them in Atlantic City, some of them sought out a Sunday worship service. The First Presbyterian Church, located near the Boardwalk at 1013 Pacific Avenue, was often filled on Sunday. Although there were over thirty churches in the turn-of-the-century city, many of the Sunday visitors found outlets for their religious inclinations along the Boardwalk. The Victoria Hotel offered an open-air religious service, while Applegate's Pier featured "Sunday night sacred concerts." John L. Young and Stewart R. McShay converted the organ that accompanied their carousel to perform sacred music on Sundays. Handing out hymn books to the crowds, they announced, "Church services as usual at the merry-go-round on Sunday afternoon."

The wooden church building has since been supplanted by a substantial brownstone church that has taken on a new mission in recent years. When Jean Webster, a casino chef, came across a homeless man foraging for food, she began feeding indigents in her home. With help from the Friends of Jean Webster, she established a soup kitchen at First Presbyterian Church. Sister Jean and her volunteers serve lunch to as many as 600 people a day—and more than 1,000 on holidays. The casinos donate their kitchen leftovers to help the cause, and celebrities in town often stop by to pitch in. One of Atlantic City's famous blue jitneys can be seen next to the church. Although some hotels provided transportation for their guests, jitney drivers began to comb the streets for customers as early as 1915. They charged a "jitney," slang for "nickel," for a ride. Young Mario Lanza's only nonmusical job was to drive an Atlantic City jitney. Fortunately for the passengers, he sang as he drove. Unfortunately for him, he neglected to collect fares and was fired.

Nineteenth-century residents of Atlantic City might not have noticed the year-to-year changes made by the Atlantic Ocean to the contours of their island. A look at a succession of maps, however, reveals startling shifts in surprisingly short periods. One 1877 map of the city shows a wide arc of sandy beach stretching south from New Jersey Avenue to Georgia Avenue, which was nonexistent when the island was mapped in 1852. The Absecon Lighthouse—originally a full three blocks from both the Atlantic Ocean to its east and the

Absecon Inlet to its north when it was built in 1856—was a few yards from the waves by 1877. The city quickly constructed four wood and stone jetties so that by the 1880s sand had begun to fill in the spaces between the jetties, thereby pushing the Atlantic Ocean away from the base of the lighthouse. This circa-1900 photograph shows one section of the Boardwalk on a diagonal run to the Inlet. In the distance is a new section of the Boardwalk being built to match the new contour of the island, reclaimed from the sea.

The land at this corner of Atlantic City has been preserved by the system of stone breakers that have kept the Atlantic Ocean at bay for a century. The large building on the left is the Flagship, part of the Fantasea Resorts complex. It overlooks the section of the Boardwalk where the famous Hackney's was once located. Harry Hackney opened a clam stand in 1912 that grew into a legendary seafood restaurant. Specializing in lobster, it could serve 3,200 diners at a single sitting—and there were still customers lined up at the door. The headquarters for Atlantic City's jitneys is also nearby. These thirteen-passenger minibuses are available twenty-four hours a day. One of America's only privately run bus services, they move swiftly from one end of the city to the other, mainly on Pacific Avenue. One casino-subsidized jitney service carries passengers for free from the Atlantic City Rail Terminal to each of the casinos.

Famed inventor Thomas Edison often found himself in Atlantic City. It was not only one of the earliest cities to employ his electrical lighting system, but it also put his patented formula for reinforced concrete to use. The exotic Blenheim Hotel was the first building in the world to be built from Edison's concrete, and he personally supervised the process. Edison also designed the concrete foundation for this house at 622 North Connecticut Avenue. Homes with concrete slabs were being promoted in the early 1900s for seashore construction as an alternative to the standard foundation of pilings. The Lambie Concrete House Corporation claimed that they were "warm, dry, and vermin-proof." This summer house with concrete walls was originally the residence of Edison's friend Jacob Blaw, an inventor who was himself involved in concrete construction.

Gardner's Basin, which flows directly behind the house, may be the reason the house's foundation and concrete slab list as much as 15 percent. Now up for sale, the building's chances of long-term survival are diminishing by the day. The Casino Reinvestment Development Authority spent $20,000 for improvements in 2001, in the hopes of stabilizing the historic building. Unfortunately, it did not place its normal deed restriction on the property, which would have prevented the owner from selling or demolishing it. For sale at the time this photo was taken, it has been described by the Fealtor as an "uninhabitable shack: the inside is like a funhouse." Although the house is considered architecturally significant, it is not listed as an official landmark by New Jersey—a designation that might save it from the wrecker's ball.

The Atlantic City Coast Guard Station was built at the junction of Clam Creek and Absecon Inlet in 1941. The Coast Guard traces its history to 1790, when Congress authorized the building of ten cutters (fast ships) to patrol the coast. The responsibility of the Revenue Cutter Service was to enforce the tariff and trade laws, and prevent smuggling. The Life-Saving Service, with its main station at the base of the Absecon Lighthouse, was one of the earliest such services in the nation. New Jersey's network of Life-Saving Stations was also the most extensive. In 1915 the Revenue Cutter Service officially merged with the Life-Saving Service. In 1939 the U.S. Lighthouse Service was also transferred to the United States Coast Guard—giving the nation a single coordinated organization for protecting the coast.

The fifty-two active-duty men and women at the Atlantic City Coast Guard Station are responsible for 250 square miles of ocean and bays, and perform 400 search-and-rescue missions a year. The area behind the station, mainly undeveloped marshland, is now the most dramatically changed section of Atlantic City. Rising beyond the Coast Guard Station are the hotel towers for the Trump Marina Hotel Casino and the Borgata. The two golden towers belong to the Borgata, the most successful casino in Atlantic City. The glitzy

Borgata features luxurious spas, five pools, an enormous casino floor with a new eighty-five-table poker room, and restaurants run by celebrity chefs Wolfgang Puck, Michael Mina, and Bobby Flay. Inspired by Borgata's track record as a magnet for celebrities and high rollers, MGM Mirage has announced plans for a $5 billion resort in the Marina District. It is expected to contain a 280,000-square-foot casino and three hotel towers, including a fifty-seven-story skyscraper—the tallest in New Jersey.

When the Camden and Atlantic Railroad Company laid its first set of tracks to Atlantic City in 1854, it also ran a set of tracks up Atlantic Avenue, curving northwest to end at the Inlet. There, it erected a pavilion that afforded the ladies a place to listen to concert bands while they waited for their gentlemen to return from fishing excursions. In the late 1800s, without universal refrigeration, the Inlet was a good place to find a fresh fish dinner. It was also this northern end of Absecon Island that attracted the majority of vacationers in the first decades of the city. The Inlet Amusement Park advertised Gleason, King of Horse Trainers, featuring "Exciting Contests with Wild and Vicious Animals." The 1880s inset photo shows the throngs crowded in the surf during the bathing hour. The men's rented suits consisted of shirts and bathing pants down to the knees. The women wore large straw hats and three layers of black bathing attire.

Gardner's Basin is now the name of the waterfront park created at the northern end of the Inlet. Atlantic City has not had a large commercial fishing fleet since the 1960s, but excursion boats are available for sport fishing, speedboat rides, and sightseeing cruises. One particularly successful attraction is the Atlantic City Aquarium—a family-friendly institution that attracts 14,000 people annually. The new forty-seven-story hotel tower of

Harrah's can be seen in the distance. Harrah's offers extensive buffets, a food court, and a large retail complex, as well as new entertainment outlets. The Farley State Marina across Clam Creek is the most extensive docking area in Atlantic City, offering 640 floating boat slips ready for yachts as long as 300 feet. Managed by Trump Marina Associates, it features a ship's store, the Deck (a bayfront bar and nightclub), and the Harbor View gourmet restaurant.

In 1854, Jonathan Pitney, Atlantic City's founding father, convinced the U.S. Lighthouse Service to build a lighthouse on the high dunes at the northern end of Absecon Island near the mouth of the inlet. By 1856, the 167-foot Absecon Lighthouse, New Jersey's tallest, was completed under the direction of Lieutenant George Meade, who would later command the Union army at Gettysburg. The light in the lantern was thrown nearly twenty miles out to sea through its enormous thirty-six-plate custom-made Fresnel lens. Kerosene was the original fuel, but incandescent oil lamps were used beginning in 1910, followed by electric lights in 1925. The lighthouse keeper had to climb 228 steps to the top. Although the bricks gave the Absecon Lighthouse its own uniform redbrick color during the first decade of operation, they were later painted in large bands of white and red. Each of the lighthouses along the New Jersey shore had its own colors, or "daymark," so that ships could tell how far they had traveled along the coast. No longer functional for maritime safety, the Absecon Lighthouse was decommissioned in 1933.

Neglected except for ceremonial lightings to mark historical occasions, the Absecon Lighthouse was finally included in both the New Jersey and National Register of Historic Places by 1971. The Inlet Public/Private Association was formed in 1988 and began to press for funds to restore the lighthouse. The lighthouse is now restored, thanks to funds from the city, state, and Casino Reinvestment Development Authority. With an executive director and a restored keeper's house, the Absecon Lighthouse, at 31 South Rhode Island Avenue, is now open for individual and group tours. It also offers a variety of educational programs related to sailing, lifesaving, and Atlantic City history.

Atlantic City was not the first to spread boards on the beach as a walkway, but it was the first city in the world to lay a grand wooden boulevard stretching for miles along the sea. Its initial effort in 1870 was a raised walkway only ten feet wide and eighteen inches above the sand dunes. This Boardwalk was the site for the first Boardwalk Easter Parade, which took place on April 16, 1876. It was organized to attract some of the huge crowds traveling to Philadelphia for the great Centennial Exhibition. America's first successful world's fair, the Centennial Exhibition drew over 25 percent of the nation's population—a healing event after the Civil War. The third Boardwalk, seen in this rare photograph, is particularly interesting. This time the city built the walk five feet above the beach. At the end of each block, where the Boardwalk crossed an avenue, the wooden walk was raised high enough to allow a horse or covered wagon to pass underneath. Riding horses on the beach was a popular pastime.

The Boardwalk was declared an official Atlantic City street in 1896. Since 1902 the city has controlled a sixty-foot-wide right-of-way, although the Boardwalk uses this full width for less than two miles of its length. The northernmost section alongside the inlet is twenty feet wide. The section that curves from Absecon Inlet around to the Atlantic Ocean is forty feet wide. From Massachusetts Avenue to Bellevue Avenue, the Boardwalk is at its full sixty-foot width, as seen here. The modern Boardwalk is supposed to be ten feet above the beach. In practice, it averages eleven feet in height. Property owners along the Boardwalk may build very close to the wooden walkway, but their structures cannot be directly attached. Atlantic City itself lies about eight feet above sea level, which keeps it five feet above the mean high-water mark. With so much coastline, New Jersey has refined its building codes to ensure reasonable protection for people and property.

These proud, hardy men had one mission: to watch for ships in distress and attempt to rescue the crews and passengers. The early name for the inlet at the northern end of Absecon Island was Graverods Inlet (a version of "graveyard"), named for the frequency of the shipwrecks on this treacherous section of the Jersey shore. Before Atlantic City was even incorporated, a ship salvager, Ryon Adams, set up a lookout for ships on the island. His house was constructed of wood salvaged from the wreck of the ship *Lovenia*. In 1849

New Jersey's first official Life-Saving Station was established near the beach at what would become Connecticut Avenue, the Government Boat House. By 1871, professional Life Saving Service crews manned the main station next to the Absecon Lighthouse and added two more, including one on Annapolis Avenue, shown here in this 1890s photo. The tower with its rescue boats is a full two blocks from the shore. In an emergency, horses or men in harness would haul the boat to the beach.

This house is still rescuing people—not shipwrecked sailors, but infants and children. The noble tradition began very early in Atlantic City when Philadelphia philanthropists founded the Children's Seashore House to provide "sea air and bathing . . . beneficial for certain types of diseases, especially where children are the patients." It was one of the very few sites in the city that served all invalid children regardless of race, residence, or ability to pay. The first Children's Seashore House was a handsome building erected right on the shore in 1873, where the Blenheim Hotel would later be built. The Children's Seashore House was closed for renovations at the time of the photograph. It is soon to reopen as the Providence Seashore House, a pediatric daycare center for infants through age five. Children with mild impairments will be cared for by a highly trained staff, including a doctor, a nurse, and a dietician. Atlantic City's tradition of rescuing people in distress and caring for children with special needs continues to this day.

This photograph of the Atlantic City Tuna Club on fire was taken on February 6, 1946. The fishing club grew out of the Atlantic City Yacht Club—the organization originally formed around the Inlet pier. Men's fishing clubs, like the West Side Fishing Club at North Missouri Avenue in Atlantic City, were popular along the Jersey coast. Members docked both private boats and charter fishing boats at the club. The Atlantic City Tuna Club also kept homing pigeons, which the fishermen would take aboard their boats. If they ran into trouble at sea, or simply wanted to get a message back to the mainland, they would send a note via carrier pigeon. When Atlantic City was first settled, the Inlet area was shallow marshland. It was dug out in the 1870s and 1880s to allow boats to dock.

The two cedar-shake houses with boat garages, seen on the left, are called the Smith Estate Houses. They reputedly had metal rails running into the water so that rum-running boats could be hauled up the rails, inside and out of sight of the authorities. These houses have undergone excellent historic restorations. Although there is no expectation that a large commercial fishing fleet and the necessary packing houses will ever return to Atlantic City, the Inlet area is becoming home to a burgeoning number of yachts and private boats. The fastest-developing docking area is in the water nearest the Marina District casinos on the northern side of the Inlet, the Senator Frank S. Farley State Marina.

The most dramatic act on Steel Pier was the high-diving horse. It would clamber up a ramp forty feet in the air. Once at the top, a rider would mount the horse and grab the harness just before the horse's front hooves edged over the small platform. Each animal had its own rhythm; some dove immediately, while others took a slower pace. As the crowd held its breath, horse and rider plunged into a twelve-foot pool of water. Lorena Carver was one of the first to ride the diving horse. Claiming that it was not as hard as it looked, she once observed, "All the girl has to do is look pretty and not fear height or water." It was critical for the rider to bury her head near the base of the horse's neck as they plunged into the pool. Lorena's sister-in-law, Sonora Carver, went blind after her retinas detached when she hit the water the wrong way. She continued to perform the stunt for eleven years, listening for the horse's gait as it approached the ramp to time her leap onto its back. The inset photo shows Sonora on Red Lips.

Donald Trump purchased the fire-devastated Steel Pier as an extension of his Taj Mahal Casino complex and rebuilt it—this time on concrete pilings. In 1993 he leased the pier to the Catanoso brothers, who had grown up on Jersey shore rides. Trump apparently hoped that the Steel Pier would keep the kids occupied, freeing up their parents to spend the big bucks inside the casino. The Catanosos introduced a version of the classic diving horse act.

A pony without a rider would dive thirty feet into a pool eight feet deep. Objections from animal-rights groups put an end to this spectacle after one season. Although the Steel Pier cannot match large-scale amusement parks, the Catanoso brothers take pride in providing the public with unique, high-quality rides. The Crazy Mouse has been rated as one of the top steel coasters in the country. Along with the Slingshot, it's a guaranteed high-tech thrill ride.

Atlantic City's piers were a world's fair of amusements—everything from opera stars and marching bands to exotic civilizations in native dress. Along with staged catastrophes like the Johnstown Flood, several of the piers offered acrobatics and animal acts. The Steel Pier was certainly the prime place for daredevil and circus acts. Next to the diving horse, the most famous—and most dangerous—was the human cannonball. Sometimes a single man was shot from the great cannon at the end of the pier, as seen in this 1935 photo. During one period, two brothers known as the "Flying Zachinis" were fired simultaneously, an especially tricky feat. One woman, Mademoiselle Alexme, was also shot from the cannon. In fact, because she lost a labor dispute with the Steel Pier, she was sentenced to be fired out of the cannon three times a day.

The most thrilling ride on the Steel Pier today features no animals—just two civilians strapped to an open metal frame and then slung skyward. Tony Catanoso and his brothers were the first to introduce the Slingshot to the United States. Before it was installed at the Steel Pier, it was improved with additional safety and redundancy features. The Catanosos had rides custom-made for the pier. Their beautifully appointed Ferris wheel was imported from Italy. They commissioned a unique double-decker carousel decorated with images of old Atlantic City. Exotic scenes that matched the Taj Mahal Casino were also incorporated in the design.

The buildings along the Boardwalk from Pennsylvania to Delaware avenues include the States Avenue Opera House with its Moorish silhouette, but it is the forms on the beach that capture the viewer's attention. The bathing attire in this scene has come a long way from the earlier centuries of skinny-dipping Lenape Indians. The inset photo reveals the type of bathing attire worn on the beach in the 1890s, when stripes were in vogue. Full Victorian garb included ankle-length pantaloons and several sets of undergarments. Women's bathing skirts had become somewhat shorter and more form-fitting by the time that the main photo was taken, some twenty years later. Women could take their recommended two or three—but no more than fifteen—minutes' dip in the surf with more freedom. It was decades before they discarded the stockings and began to wear single-piece swimsuits.

One of Atlantic City's newest oceanfront casinos, the Showboat Hotel and Casino (the tall building with the raked front at the center of the photo) opened in March of 1987. In an attempt to make its resort more welcoming to families, it featured a bowling alley. Resorts Atlantic City actually owns the land, charging Showboat $6.4 million per year on a ninety-nine-year lease. The Showboat was the first casino in the city to have a poker room and to offer keno. It was also the first to provide horse-racing simulcasts. The Showboat boasts special House of Blues–themed suites in its Orleans Tower, as well as Mardi Gras suites with beach views and wraparound balconies. Its House of Blues nightclub, cofounded by Dan Aykroyd, offers an edgy mix of rap, rock, and blues artists. The Showboat is getting a new neighbor, Revel Entertainment's twin forty-eight-story hotel towers. With 170,000 square feet of casino space and buildings twice the height of the Showboat, this complex will bookend the northern end of the Boardwalk.

One of Atlantic City's first opera houses was built on the Boardwalk at States Avenue. Its distinctive and somewhat Moorish facade stands out in many photographs of the early Boardwalk. In 1899, the London Ghost Show was the entertainment at the States Avenue Opera House. Although the opera houses occasionally featured classical vocal entertainment, more frequently they showcased vaudeville productions, animal acts, staged disasters, and sporting events. In fact, a close look at the facade reveals an advertisement for a boxing match. Disasters like the destruction of Herculaneum, the Johnstown flood, and Custer's last stand were popular entertainment. The stages at the northern end of the Boardwalk in the late 1800s and early 1900s, like the States Avenue Opera House, presented "family vaudeville," as opposed to more bawdy variety acts. The latter were clustered closer to the southern end, near the beer gardens.

Size matters at Donald Trump's Taj Mahal. The casino floor is the size of four football fields. It has just opened a new $5 million baccarat and high-end gaming pit. Its original hotel tower, which reaches fifty-one stories, will soon be paired with a new 800-room tower. The lavish penthouse suites boast bathrooms as large as guest rooms, enormous living rooms with the best appointments, and dining rooms with domed ceilings. Even these suites are dwarfed by the 4,500-square-foot Alexander the Great suite, complete with wet bar, private exercise room, and grand piano. Although the palaces in India were originally built for royalty, now even the commoners can dine on the "Sultan's Feast" or eat at the New Delhi Deli. As the Taj's telephone operators like to greet callers, "Thank you for calling the Trump Taj Mahal, where wonders never cease."

It is a testament to the faith of the Camden and Atlantic Land Company investors that, while they were laying tracks from Philadelphia to Atlantic City, they were also building the United States Hotel—with 600 rooms, the largest in the nation. A private set of rails ran two blocks from the hotel straight to the beach. Guests were transported in horse-drawn rail cars to the hotel's seaside bathhouses. The United States Hotel was still under construction when it greeted the first railroad cars crowded with investors and newsmen on July 1, 1854. Even so, it managed to serve a full dinner for the 600 guests. President Ulysses S. Grant stayed at the hotel on July 25, 1874. One observer claimed that "Grant drank so much . . . that he probably doesn't remember being here." The guests at the United States Hotel were also besieged by other heavy drinkers: greenhead flies, gnats, and mosquitoes. They so tormented the horses at the hotel that one team "ran away demolishing the carriage, and broke the arm of one of the ladies."

The narrow lane used for the United States Hotel's private rail line to the beach was eventually converted to United States Avenue, and finally to States Avenue. Now all that remains is the name, because the Showboat has obliterated the actual street with its own casino hotel. With one of the largest slots floors in Atlantic City, the Showboat is a magnet for tour buses. Auto drivers park either in the parking lot where the United States Hotel once stood or across the street in the huge parking deck provided by the Showboat. The Pacific Avenue end of the deck has been decorated like a Mississippi riverboat.

The original 1869 Haddon House was a prefab hotel built by a lumberyard in Haddonfield, New Jersey. The fitted lumber was shipped by rail to Atlantic City and assembled fifty feet from the ocean's storm tide. Twenty years later, tides had moved the waterline 1,000 feet farther from the hotel, so the building was moved closer. This circa 1900 photograph shows Haddon House in its new location, graced by the arches of its distinctive arcade, newly added to the Boardwalk side. In 1929 the hotel was replaced with a much larger 600-room brick-and-concrete building (inset). During World War II, Haddon House served as one of the world's largest military hospitals, providing new limbs manufactured in its basement shop for over 5,000 amputees. Many of the soldiers returned after the war as tourists, some of them to marry local girls who had attended their convalescence. Rolling chairs were first used in Philadelphia to help people navigate the 100-plus buildings at the 1876 Centennial Exposition, but it was Atlantic City's Boardwalk that made it a tradition.

The vote to legalize gambling in New Jersey passed in 1976. Two years before, prompted by a coalition of politicians and church groups called No Dice, the measure had gone down to a resounding defeat. An early financial supporter of the 1976 bill, Resorts International had a year's head start on any other casino. Haddon House was quickly rehabbed to include a gambling floor, but left with enough hotel rooms to meet the Casino Control Act's regulations—a minimum of 500. Resorts opened its doors to eager gamblers on May 28, 1978. In its first

220 days, Resorts grossed over $134 million, more than any other casino in the world. The casino revived Atlantic City's showbiz tradition, selecting promoter Frank Gelb to manage the entertainment. He booked mainly sports events and boxing matches, until someone asked him to do something for someone named Pavarotti. Gelb said, "I asked how much he weighed. I thought Pavarotti was a fighter." The great tenor became the first of many musical spectaculars at the Resorts showroom, and a poker partner of Gelb's.

This early 1900s photo shows the Atlantic City Beach Patrol in front of their "hospital tent" on the beach at South Carolina Avenue. This tent, donated and supplied by Johnson & Johnson, served as a first aid station for people rescued by the patrol, the first professional lifeguard corps in America. Atlantic City's first "constable of the surf" was appointed in 1855. William S. Cazier was paid $117 to work through the summer. Soon regular members of the police force joined the constables in patrolling the beach. From 11:00 a.m. to 1:30 p.m., they wore swimming garb. Many beachfront hotels also provided private lifeguards. Captain William Street patented a set of "Life Lines for Surf Bathing": metal cables attached to masts on the beach run into the water to anchors beyond the roiling surf. Lines were hung every nine feet from the cables for ocean bathers to grab and avoid being swept out to sea.

The headquarters of the Atlantic City Beach Patrol at South Carolina Avenue is still referred to by locals as the "lifeguard tent." Atlantic City has such confidence in its lifeguards that leadership on the beach has sometimes translated into political office. Applicants for America's first professional lifeguard service must undergo rigorous training and testing. Atlantic City also hosts the World Championship Ocean Marathon Swim—an annual swim around Absecon Island in July. Spectators in Atlantic City, Ventnor, and Margate cheer on the contestants as they forge ahead in this grueling competition that can take eight or nine hours.

Extra Dry, located on the northern end of Atlantic Avenue, boasted both "Ladies and Gentlemen's Dining Parlors." It served not only hard liquor, but dry imported wines. Women who guarded their reputations had to be choosy about the restaurants they frequented. Tourist brochures for Atlantic City extolled the respectability of the resort, as in this 1904 claim: "Visitors, ladies or gentlemen, singly or together, may pass and loiter at all times of the day and evening in perfect safety, free from intoxication annoyance and without danger of being spoken to by other than their friends." A more jaded observer pointed out the dangerous influence of the resort, where women who never went to anything more exciting than "an ice cream sociable" back home gradually lost their inhibitions and would "become acquainted with some man who sits at the same table with her . . . in less than a week she will be visiting 'grottoes' with him in the evening, and drinking highballs."

The building is still there, now proclaiming "Oriental Massage." At the moment, however, it stands vacant. Always a part of the Atlantic City scene, some nineteenth-century shops advertised Swedish massage. The modern city is practically an epicenter for massage, from the luxurious spas of the casinos to the storefront massage parlors along the Boardwalk. The casinos boast marble facilities, aromatherapy, health clubs, and even beachside cabanas.

The stores offer chair, water and deep-tissue massages. Like most resorts, Atlantic City has massage services of every type. Although restaurants and drinking establishments may have been the barometers of respectability for women in nineteenth-century Atlantic City, the city's massage industry may serve as a filter for today's male visitors to the resort.

One of Atlantic City's most ornate vintage structures does not preside over the Boardwalk; the Bartlett Building is located on Atlantic Avenue within the city's residential and commercial heart. It is in fact two buildings. The original two-story building with its central cupola and clock was still situated on the corner of North Carolina Avenue and Atlantic Avenue while the "new" building was under construction. The original was then eased around the corner on rolling logs to permit the completion of the six-story Bartlett Building up to the corner. The original Bartlett Building was then attached as a wing of the new one in 1903. Over time, the new building experienced its own changes, surrendering its beautiful Seth Thomas tower clock so that an additional floor could be added to the structure.

For many years, the new seventh floor housed Atlantic City's courtrooms. There are still court connections. L & L Court Reporting occupies a large suite in the building. It not only trains court reporters but also offers special high-resolution videoconferencing for litigation. Several law firms have offices in the building. One of them has occupied the building for half a century—the law firm of Wallen and Wallen. The office has passed from father to son. In fact, the current Wallen's grandfather was one of Atlantic

City's premier architects. The largest single building occupant is Cooper Levenson, a law firm with lengthy ties to the city and the Bartlett Building. Their staff not only fills the "old" building, but it has several floors of the "new" one as well. Like so many other corporations in Atlantic City, Cooper Levenson has the biggest game in town as a client: the gaming industry. In fact, Levenson helped spearhead the successful drive to pass New Jersey's casino bill.

Kuehnle's Hotel and City Hall, Atlantic City, N. J.

Louis Kuehnle became the manager of his family's hotel on Atlantic Avenue at the corner of South Carolina when he was only eighteen. The City Hall tower, just down the street, can be seen on the left. In 1893, Kuehnle built a four-story building of stores and apartments that he rented out to expanding city departments, in time dubbed the "annex." By 1900 he had become Atlantic City's first political boss. No city employee, candidate, or contract was approved without the okay of "Commodore" Louis Kuehnle. Kuehnle ran Atlantic City's Republican Party, holding the organizational meetings at his hotel, nicknamed "the Corner." His main source of income was protection money paid by the gambling rooms, brothels, and saloons, as well as a cut of the fees collected by the sheriff's office: summonses, foreclosures, and housing prisoners. One newspaper complained: "The gambling saloons are running in full blast. The Mayor . . . answers not a word. The Chief of Police says that he has been ill . . . Meanwhile the ivory chips clink merrily."

One of the first great Atlantic City masters of the art of the deal, Commodore Kuehnle could take satisfaction in the realization that his handsome four-story modern office building is still a hotbed of negotiations and transactions. Built originally as the headquarters for the Boardwalk National Bank, it is now occupied by Wachovia National Bank—one of America's largest, thanks to mergers with First Union and CoreStates. The largest suite of offices is occupied by the national law firm Fox and Rothschild. Founded over a century ago in Philadelphia, it has branches from New York to Los Angeles. Many of its staff in the Atlantic City office specialize in gaming industry matters. The Revel Corporation, which is erecting an immense new casino complex near Park Place and the Boardwalk, also has offices here.

In 1920, 168 shows opened at three theaters in Atlantic City: the Globe, the Woods, and Nixon's Apollo Theatre. Atlantic City had become the chief tryout city for Broadway plays. Marie Dressler opened in *Tillie's Nightmare* at the Apollo on March 1. It was soon followed by an Irish musical that had everyone singing "When Irish Eyes Are Smiling" and "My Wild Irish Rose." Victor Herbert composed an operetta for an April 3 opening. The Ziegfeld Follies later took over the theater, with Helen Hayes starring in a play during August. Tallulah Bankhead, the Shuberts, Paul Whiteman, Fred Astaire, Jeanette MacDonald—they were all part of the Atlantic City show scene. On October 28, 1924, the largest pre-Broadway musical production ever held opened at the Apollo, with a cast of 150—Sigmund Romberg's *The Student Prince in Heidelberg*. The New York and Philadelphia theater critics loved it. When it opened in New York City with its new title, *The Student Prince*, it became an international smash.

The most dramatic event on this spot is probably the moment the guests at the Atlantic Palace open the door to their twenty-eighth-floor suite and take in the breathtaking view of the Atlantic Ocean. At the Boardwalk level, the drama comes from the Belrose Galleries to the right of the Atlantic Palace's entrance. Larger-than-life bronze figures practically leap out at Boardwalk strollers, beckoning tourists to explore the depths of the store. The aisles are crowded with antiques, reproductions, European tapestries, and chess sets depicting a world of conflicts. It is a seamless transition to step from the Boardwalk into the adjacent stores, but what the shoppers cannot see is that none of these buildings are structurally connected to the Boardwalk. They all have their own supporting beams and walls and the responsibility to maintain them. The Casino Reinvestment Development Authority does provide funds for facade improvements, but each participating commercial establishment must also contribute a percentage of the costs.

This may be the earliest known photograph of the world's first Ferris wheel. William Somers built the first such wheel in 1891 in Atlantic City, and followed that feat by erecting what he called his "Observation Roundabout" in Asbury Park and then Coney Island. He was apparently negotiating to erect a large wheel as a featured ride at Chicago's 1893 Columbian Exposition when the planners sent the young engineer George Washington Gale Ferris to Atlantic City. He carefully examined Somers's invention and returned to Chicago. There he built an enormous steel wheel and named it for himself; it was the hit of the fair. William Somers had patented his construction, so he sued Ferris. The case was still under review when Ferris died, but it was his name immortalized by the wheel. Some purists still claim that it should be called the "Somers wheel."

This modern row of stores is perhaps the best example on the Boardwalk of the facade renewal accomplished by the Casino Reinvestment Development Authority. The restored exterior of the Stanley Theatre with its marquee can be seen in the distance (center left), the James' Salt Water Taffy store—looking much the way it did a century ago—is in the center right, and JP Imports is at the right edge of the photo. JP features sports souvenirs and figurines of cartoon characters, soldiers, classic Greek statues like the Venus de Milo, and even nativity scenes. The proprietors named their store JP Imports in honor of Dada J. P. Vaswani, the Hindu holy man and apostle of nonviolence, revered by many around the world for his spiritual writings. Curiously, although Greek gods and Christian statues are available, there are no figures of Vishnu, the elephant-headed Ganesh, or Shiva for sale. There is, however, in the glass display case of fine Lenox china, one charming Ferris . . . correction, Somers wheel.

Brode's Baths was one of several dozen bathhouses in early Atlantic City, most of them featuring hot and cold seawater pools. They also rented bathing costumes. Alfred Heston's Victorian-era tourist brochures insisted that the rental garments would provide ladies with full privacy: "Special care has been taken in the selection of material and in the making of secure comfort and freedom from annoyance by faulty seams or fastenings. Everything of an immodest character is strictly avoided." Atlantic City promoted itself as a wintertime resort, warmer than other parts of the northeastern United States. One railroad promotional pamphlet described this idyllic scene: "Even in midwinter . . . sojourners at Atlantic City are lolling on the sands, reveling in glorious sunlight, and drinking in deep draughts of the strength-creating air." Not much lolling was going on after the great blizzard of March 1888 dumped several feet of snow on the Boardwalk (inset).

When Robert Leroy Ripley honeymooned in Atlantic City with his bride Beatrice in 1919, he probably would not have believed it if someone told him there would be a Ripley's Believe It or Not! Museum on the Boardwalk a century later. Ripley had begun his world travels in 1914 with a trip to Europe. By the time he opened his first "odditorium" in Chicago in 1933, this modern Marco Polo had visited 200 countries and traveled over 100,000 miles. He covered 24,000 miles on just one trip, including 8,000 by ship and 1,000 by camel and donkey. Ripley's Believe It or Not! Museum in Atlantic City is one of nearly thirty around the globe—from Lancashire, England, to Makmur, Malaysia. Each one features items from Ripley's own enormous collection of artifacts. Shrunken heads, five-legged animals, pictures of a man eight feet, eleven inches tall, exotic treasures, the Mona Lisa made out of toast, to name a few. Of course, they all contain Ripley's popular cartoons describing the strange customs and oddities he found.

St. James African Methodist Episcopal Church was the first traditional black church in Atlantic City. Founded in 1875 by Reverend Jeremiah H. Pierce, Bethel African Methodist Episcopal Church was renamed St. James in 1884 when it was moved to its present location at New York and Arctic avenues. In 1910, two castlelike towers were added to the front facade and the original frame building was clad in brick, a mark of the congregation's success. The "Church with an Open Door" has been a leader throughout the history of Atlantic City's African American community. In conjunction with the Board of Trade, an organization of black businesspeople, it hosted a variety of conferences in Atlantic City. African Americans, often excluded from mainstream political and commercial networks, found in their churches a primary source of support. A rich array of clubs, organizations, and youth groups were sponsored by the churches. By 1950, Atlantic City's African American residents had fourteen churches from which to choose.

Currently undergoing restoration, St. James Church has plans to replace its signature beacon domes. The church remains a vibrant force in the community. Leaders from St. James have been at the forefront of the transformation of Atlantic City into a more democratic and inclusive place. For the past forty years, St. James has been the site for the annual Atlantic City NAACP Martin Luther King Jr. Celebration. The pastor and congregation blend traditional church organizations with new programs that address current community needs. Bright's Villas, 141 units of affordable housing, and CHILL, a youth reading and life-skills program, are examples of the church's community outreach.

Atlantic City's first casino did not feature gambling tables. It contained a sun deck, swimming pool, bowling alley, and dance floor. While some of the gentlemen in this upper-class establishment may have enjoyed cards and cigars, the building was really designed to afford women as well as men a place for healthy seashore diversions. The casino was erected in 1892 at Indiana Avenue and the Boardwalk, with an enclosed walkway that ran the 500-foot length of Brighton Park to the exclusive Brighton Hotel. Acquired in a fit of resentment by a Philadelphia millionaire who had found his favorite Atlantic City hotel completely booked one summer, the Brighton admitted only other members of Philadelphia's Main Line. Instead of the usual hackneys, the hotel sent its own full coach drawn by four horses to meet guests at the train station. It charged up to $5 a day for a room, the highest rates in the city. This circa 1905 photo shows the newly erected fifth Boardwalk. Built in 1896 on wooden pilings ten feet above the beach, it had metal railings for the safety of strollers.

The combined effect of a foggy night and the turn-of-the-century streetlamps hearken back to the Boardwalk of old. Atlantic City has always been "turned on," as its slogan claims, but there was a certain charm and romance in the city's early lighting schemes. In an era when some modern buildings are so blanketed with lights that they produce a kind of light pollution, one of the Boardwalk Revitalization's goals is to return to more selective lighting.

Although the Brighton Casino is no longer here, there are plenty of other casinos eager to welcome tourists. Unfortunately, some of them present a virtual blank wall to the Boardwalk, offering very limited points of access. The Casino Reinvestment Development Authority has taken the initiative to transform sections of the Boardwalk so that they will provide friendlier faces to pedestrians.

Richard Bew's Old Reliable Bath Houses may seem austere by modern standards, but this establishment was a significant improvement on the original crude sheds. In the 1860s, barkers would drag them to the beach at the start of the season, and then haul them back up into the dunes in the fall. For twenty-five cents, visitors could use the sheds to change into rented beach clothes. After their time in the surf, they returned to the bathhouses. They were handed a bucket of salt water to wash the sand off their limbs.

After changing back into their regular clothes, they would return to the railroad station. Once the Boardwalk was built, more permanent structures supplanted the portable bathhouses. This 1880s photo shows the third Boardwalk, which had a hump at the intersection of each avenue to permit horses to reach the beach. The inset shows Booth's Restaurant, around the corner, serving up circa-1900 fast food.

A wooden street is, of course, more susceptible to fire than the average avenue; and, since most of the bathhouses were of necessity built close to the Boardwalk, many of them went up in flames. Those that survived fire were eventually supplanted by the amenities provided in the hotels. For some reason, this Boardwalk section near Illinois and New York avenues has experienced more than its share of fires. One occurred in 1892, followed by a particularly devastating fire in 1902 that took out fifteen hotels. This section has set off the fire alarms as recently as 2006. Although a very dense, fire-retardant wood now covers the Boardwalk, the large four-by-fourteen-inch timbers that support the deck are still southern yellow pine. Store owners and pier managers alike can take consolation in knowing that the Boardwalk is so strong that, for much of its length from New Jersey to Albany avenues, it can support a 60,000-pound fire truck.

An 1870 city council resolution stated that "the city build a board walk along the beach … 10 feet wide; that the boards be laid lengthwise." Alexander Boardman, a conductor on the first railroad, and Jacob Keim, a boarding home proprietor, made the original proposition in 1870 to line the edge of the beach with boards, so that the fine carpets and upholstered furniture in the lobbies of the hotels and on the trains could be maintained. The city erected five different boardwalks over the next twenty-five years. Each one enlarged or improved on the previous one—rising from eighteen inches above the sand to ten feet in the 1896 walk, and from an original ten feet in width for the 1896 Boardwalk to the current width of forty to sixty feet. This 1929 photo shows the Boardwalk at full flower—the world's first, longest, and most famous wooden street.

Although the city council originally prohibited "erection of any bathhouse or shanty or building of any kind within 30 feet of the walk," it was impossible to keep the merchants and hoteliers from connecting as closely as possible to the Boardwalk. Today, as it has for a century and a half, resourceful entrepreneurs are devising every possible way to draw in the promenading public and thin out their wallets. Some Atlantic City historians like Charles E. Funnell suggest that the city actually invented "recreational shopping." After a Boardwalk stroll, with a clear sky and a rhythmic sea setting them at ease as they vacation at the shore, Atlantic City's tourists are well primed to while away a few hours in the stores and casinos that beckon them from the other side of the Boardwalk.

Diamond Jim Brady was just one of the celebrated guests to frequent the regal Shelburne Hotel, but he may have been the only one who raided the kitchen. It was not unusual for him to down three dozen oysters, two ducks, seven lobsters, and a sirloin steak for dinner, and still leave room for assorted pastries and two pounds of chocolate. He treated the love of his life, Lillian Russell, to a gold-plated bathtub in the hotel. The original Shelburne (shown above circa 1890) was a stately wooden hotel built in 1869 by Elisha Roberts, a descendant of a plain Quaker family. Roberts named his hotel in honor of a British leader who had sided with the American colonists in 1776. The family's crest on the hotel proclaimed: *Virtute non Verbis*, "Deeds, not words." The Quaker tradition of simplicity must have been sorely tried by a hotel with gold-plated bathroom fixtures in the penthouse suite. Show-business clients of the Shelburne included Victor Herbert, Al Jolson, Irving Berlin, Ethel Barrymore, and George M. Cohan, who reputedly composed the World War I anthem "Over There" during his stay in the penthouse. As shown in the main photo, the later Shelburne, which was completed in 1926, boasted a grand arched arcade facing the walk, where guests could sit in the shade and enjoy the cool ocean breezes.

Bally's used a Wild West theme for this casino, building a series of late eighteenth-century Western facades facing the Boardwalk. Visitors step from the Boardwalk into a mountain scene complete with mines, a stream, and a waterfall. Animatronic characters are panning for gold and relating stories about the West. A rattlesnake and a talking vulture add a touch of magic

realism to the scene. Occasionally a thundering storm illuminates the mountain with flashes of lightning. The gambling hall continues the Wild West theme. The casino cage is built like an old bank. Visitors play their games on old wood tables surrounded by a gun shop, a general store, a dance hall, and an undertaker. The restrooms look like abandoned mine shafts.

For the millions of Monopoly fans who can't seem to place Park Place, here it is in black and white. That small rectangular patch of park with its great fountain in the center that serves as the front lawn to the Claridge Hotel is Brighton Park. The street running the length of the park on the left side in the photo is Park Place. The Claridge is flanked by exotic Moorish hotels, the Traymore on the right and the Marlborough-Blenheim on the left. To the immediate right of the Claridge is a small hotel with a big reputation: the Brighton. This L-shaped hotel was for many years the most elegant and expensive spot in Atlantic City. In the late nineteenth century, guests who were brash enough to arrive in one of those newfangled noisy automobiles, instead of by horse-drawn coach, were refused lodging. Illinois Avenue is to the right of the Traymore, and Indiana Avenue runs next to Brighton Park, just to the right of the Claridge.

The modernized Claridge still holds court at the head of Brighton Park, but only a parking lot fills the right section of the photo where the mighty Traymore once stood. The sleek white building on the place once occupied by the Brighton, just to the right of the Claridge, is the Sands Hotel and Casino, which was imploded shortly after this photo was taken. The modern white Sands Hotel and Casino was the very first new casino building erected in Atlantic City. Other casinos had converted existing hotels to open as quickly as possible. The Sands, originally named the Brighton Hotel Casino, was completed in 1980 and soon became the favored Atlantic City spot for Sinatra and the Rat Pack. Bally's modern thirty-seven-story hotel tower, now the tallest building in the neighborhood, can be seen to the left of the Claridge. In fact, virtually everything on the left half of the photo is Bally's—including the Claridge itself. There is an enormous parking deck in the rear of Bally's that faces Pacific Avenue—the parking place.

The Hippodrome, the "world's largest ballroom," was the first building visitors encountered as they stepped onto Young's Million Dollar Pier. It served as Atlantic City's convention center until Convention Hall was erected a few blocks down the Boardwalk. In 1908 Captain John Lake Young built a three-story white Venetian palace (inset) halfway along his pier. Thomas Edison worked on the lighting for the mansion. The formal parlor featured a grand crystal chandelier from the royal palace of Vienna.

Much of the furniture was custom-made, some of it in the shape of sea creatures. Young hosted President William Howard Taft in 1911, serving the fresh fish caught in the pier's daily haul. Particularly impressive to the public as they strolled the Million Dollar Pier were the eight-foot marble statues lined up in the front yard. Imported from Florence, they revealed a great deal of the human form. Captain Young named the grandiose villa "Number One, Atlantic Ocean," and the post office honored it.

The pier nearest the Boardwalk and its grand ballroom were destroyed by fire in 1949. When it was rebuilt, it was turned into an amusement park. However, the pier never did regain the popularity of its glory years. After one abortive attempt to turn the pier into a shopping mall, Caesar's Hotel and Casino eventually purchased it. Instead of the classic marble statuary surrounding Captain Young's villa on the pier, most of the half-clad Roman statues now preside over the casino. Here guests can also enjoy elegant Roman baths, luxurious spas, and a rooftop pool. Visitors to the pier will still find one impressive bit of statuary, the fifteen-foot golden Buddha that dominates the communal table at Buddakan restaurant on the upper deck of the Pier Shops at Caesar's. The ocean end of the pier now boasts a four-story light-and-water extravaganza, the Water Show. Romantic couples can reserve the new wedding chapel, which overlooks the world's largest indoor water show. And the mailing address is still "Number One, Atlantic Ocean."

Many ships ran aground in Atlantic City, like the *Steamship Alpha* in 1890 near the Inlet (shown above). In the fierce storm of 1884, Frank Hagan climbed to the roof of a Boardwalk cigar store. Suddenly through the rain and fog, a sailor clinging to a bowsprit shouted to him: "Where am I?" The *Robert Morgan* had been flung by a huge wave onto the beach, demolishing a pier in its wake. The *New York Times* reported, "Her great black hull now rises 20 feet above the beach level. How to get her to sea again is a puzzle."

The schooner sat on the beach during the spring waiting for a high enough tide. Meanwhile, it was raking in so much money as a tourist attraction that it stayed throughout the summer. Other ships even tried to run aground on the beach to take advantage of the income, but were forced by the city to turn back. The main photograph shows the *Stafford*, which was beached in an 1894 storm near Michigan Avenue. It was moved to Texas Avenue, where a spur of the Boardwalk was constructed for the tourists.

Atlantic City merchants are still searching for ways to keep the tourists enthralled. As exciting as it might be to find a three-masted schooner sitting proudly on the sand, visitors will have to settle for surf-side cabanas these days. Despite prohibitions against setting up commercial establishments on the beach, someone has always tried to sell or rent something—whether pony rides or beach umbrellas. Most of the grand old hotels had rows of cabanas in front of their buildings. In recent years, the casinos have obtained permission to construct permanent structures on the sand. Each season they seem to grow larger and more opulent. Palm trees, wet bars, gourmet food, salsa bands, and even massage tents are being erected over sections of the sand. After decades when the casinos seemed to be turned inward, taking virtually no account of the great ocean past their Boardwalk entrances, the casinos are coming to appreciate the special allure of their environment.

Only three years after Thomas Edison masterminded America's first electrical power grid in Manhattan, lighting up eighty-five homes, Atlantic City began to light its streets with electricity. The Boardwalk was still in its early stages when it received its first string of streetlamps. Atlantic City has been America's city of lights since 1886. Trenton's R.C. Maxwell Company was responsible for some of the world's largest and most astonishing signs along the Boardwalk: the 215-foot Chesterfield sign on Steeplechase Pier and the diver slicing into the ocean in a Jantzen swimsuit. Perhaps best of all was the Seagram's racetrack sign, with four horses racing around a track every three minutes. Many a bet was made on the winner, which changed from race to race. Of course, the grand hotels also took every opportunity to intensify their nighttime glitter, as this early photo shows.

If the game of Monopoly were fully modernized, players who get stuck with the utility bill would now be able to catch a break. Atlantic City's wind farm can pump out 25 million kilowatt-hours of electricity a year. Its graceful windmills also afford a striking visual introduction to the city. The Boardwalk is still dramatically lit, perhaps even too brightly lit at some points, but it no longer monopolizes the tourists' eyes. Pacific Avenue, which was more of a back door to the grand old hotels of sixty years ago, is now a front door for many of the new casinos. Add to this the brilliantly lit casino resorts in the Marina District, and visitors may experience their best nighttime views as they drive into Atlantic City from the mainland.

Officially named the Atlantic City Auditorium, Convention Hall, seen right of center here, was a massive presence for decades. Young's Million Dollar Pier stretches 2,000 feet into the Atlantic Ocean. The large rectangular building at the far left of the photograph is the famous Ritz-Carlton Hotel, completed in 1921. In the 1920s and 1930s, Atlantic City's most powerful political boss reigned over the city. Enoch "Nucky" Johnson occupied a full floor of the Ritz, hosting lavish parties for his favorite Broadway stars, visiting entertainers, political cronies, and even America's top gangsters. Nucky rose promptly at 3:00 p.m., had a rubdown, and enjoyed his "breakfast" while looking out at the ocean: a quart of freshly squeezed orange juice, six eggs, and a ham steak. Then he would don one of his tailor-made lavender suits and head to the Boardwalk to begin his workday.

Convention Hall (now Boardwalk Hall) reigned as the largest enclosed arena in America until the modern construction of the Houston Astrodome. Casino hotels now crowd against it—although it is still an imposing and busy building. The edge of the Ritz-Carlton can just be seen at the extreme left. No longer a hotel, this graceful neo-Georgian building was modernized into luxury condominium apartments in 1982. Its elegant lobby and ballrooms have been preserved. Amenities now include a fitness room, a new pool, and a sauna. Nucky Johnson would have skipped the fitness room for the sauna. The condominium scene is a relatively new phenomenon in Atlantic City, but the New York Times sees it as a promising option for individual investors. It is especially attractive for those who like to make occasional forays into the casinos, although the condo may be the safer bet. Even though Caesar's Pier is 800 feet shorter than the original 2,000-foot Million Dollar Pier, its four stories of stores make it a massive presence on the beachfront.

Isaac N. Forrester constructed his "Epicycloidal Diversion" in 1872 at Mississippi Avenue near the Seaview Excursion House, a beach house at the end of one of the early railroad lines. This forerunner of the Ferris wheel consisted of four wheels that turned on a circular platform. Riders rotated both up and down and around the platform—an epicycloidal experience. The industrial revolution was a double-edged sword, creating new problems as it provided solutions to old ones. As Charles E. Funnell pointed out in his *By the Beautiful Sea*, the working-class tourists who visited Atlantic City on Sunday, their one day off, were escaping the smog, noise, danger, and relentlessness of their work environments that left them feeling like cogs in an industrial world. But they were using these same inventions to seek out the fresh air and relaxation of Atlantic City: a quick railroad trip to the shore, where they and their children could enjoy all sorts of inventions that spun them, twirled them, and thrilled them. The technology, which had disenfranchised them back home, was harnessed in Atlantic City for their enjoyment.

The only wheels spinning on the site of the Epicycloidal Diversion today are the roulette wheels in the Trump Plaza. Everything else is stationary—especially Vera Coking's house. Her battle a decade ago with *Penthouse* magazine publisher Bob Guccione thrust her name repeatedly into the national news. After many months of wrangling in an attempt to purchase her property, Guccione finally built the steel superstructure of his planned casino completely around her house. When Donald Trump purchased the partially finished property, he had the steel girders torn down. Now that he is planning a major expansion of the casino, Trump is engaged in his own war of words with Vera Coking. A new superstructure could be going up any day now.

The Ambassador was one of the few grand Boardwalk hotels that did not emerge from a succession of earlier wooden buildings. It was constructed in two major projects: 200 rooms in 1919, and 500 more in 1921. Begun when President Woodrow Wilson had issued a wartime restriction on liquor, it was built without a bar. Not until after Prohibition was repealed in 1933 was the elaborate Horseshoe Bar added. This great hotel played host to some of America's favorite musicians, including Isham Jones's band with Woody Herman, and Paul Whiteman with the Rhythm Boys. In fact, Whiteman may have recorded two of his top hits at the Ambassador: "Avalon" and Gershwin's "Rhapsody in Blue," the theme song for the Paul Whitman orchestra. The baritone in the Rhythm Boys was just beginning to make a name for himself in the late 1920s, Harry "Bing" Crosby. In 1929 Al Capone, Lucky Luciano, and Dutch Schultz occupied the same grand suites that had previously hosted William Jennings Bryan, Sir Arthur Conan Doyle, and the Great Caruso, who entertained audiences in the Renaissance Salon.

When Ramada Inns bought the Ambassador Hotel, they hoped to renovate it—as had Resorts International and Bally's earlier—and convert it into a casino. The New Jersey governor and the Casino Control Commission insisted that they had to start fresh. The Ambassador was demolished, except for part of the steel framework, and the new Tropicana Casino and Resort Hotel was built at the Boardwalk and Brighton Avenue. By the time it opened, it had cost almost $400 million. The holding company has since added a new 604-room hotel tower, and in 2004 another 502-room Havana Tower, a 2,400-space parking garage, and a glitzy new retail and restaurant area called the Quarter. With exciting restaurants like Cuba Libre, the Quarter has the ambience of old Havana. The Tropicana may be Atlantic City's first megaresort.

In 1881 there were fifty-three grocery stores, over 500 hotels and rooming houses, thirteen bakeries, and already thirty-one restaurants. Atlantic City was on its way to establishing a rich tradition for food lovers. The Flemish Building, built on the wedge of land where the parallel Atlantic and Pacific avenues hook into each other, was first erected in 1910. Apparently the wrong nails were used, and it was dismantled and rebuilt—opening as an exclusive men's club in 1912. Although Prohibition outlawed alcoholic beverages during the 1920s, members of the club openly flaunted the law, so the law closed them down in a surprise raid. Membership went into a slide, forcing the sale of the building to the Latz family in 1927. The Knife & Fork Inn was operated by the Latzes as a successful high-end restaurant for seventy years, attracting a devoted local following as well as celebrities like Frank Sinatra and Burt Lancaster. Mack Latz, son of the original owners, retired in his eighties, and the restaurant was closed in 1997.

It took another family with an even longer tradition in the Atlantic City restaurant business to rescue the Knife & Fork Inn. Frank, great-grandson of Harry Dougherty, who founded Dock's Oyster House in 1897, remembers biking past the Knife & Fork when he was a kid. Even then he was impressed by its distinctive architecture. In January 2005, the Dougherty family purchased the building and began an extensive renovation project. It is once again full of rich mahogany woodwork and an ornate bar that captures the feel of the pre-Prohibition days. Specializing in steaks and seafood, and boasting a 10,000-bottle wine cellar, the Knife & Fork Inn celebrates Atlantic City's century-old tradition of first-rate cuisine. Only blocks away at 2800 Atlantic Avenue is another very different Atlantic City food tradition. Tony's Baltimore Grill, with its twenty-four-hour bar, has served seafood and Italian specialties for eighty years. Its legendary pizza is celebrated by food lovers as some of the best on the East Coast.

Richard Osborn had just enough state names to apply them to the cross streets on his 1853 map of Atlantic City. The thirty-first state, California, had just been admitted to the union in 1850. Atlantic City apparently grew faster than the nation could add states. So, after Iowa Avenue, the streets were named Brighton, Morris, Chelsea, Montpelier, and Sovereign. This photograph runs from Chelsea on the right to Sovereign Avenue on the left. The Ostend Hotel is one of the few grand wooden Victorian-era hotels to be built this far south in Atlantic City. Much of this area, known as the Chelsea District, was residential. In the 1950s, the latest trend in travel lodging found room in this section—the motor inn.

Chelsea residents raised a mighty complaint to a thirty-six-floor twin-tower condominium being built between their neighborhood and the sea. One concern was the prospect that the Ocean Club would create a howling wind between its two parallel towers. The builders hired an architectural firm, which constructed a large model and had it tested in a wind tunnel. It passed, and the towers were built. With its two raked towers, the Ocean Club is Atlantic City's premier luxury condominium. It reigned for years as the largest residential high-rise on the

Atlantic coast between New Jersey and Florida. The six-story base contains an indoor pool, parking, and other public space. The towers are set back 200 feet from the Boardwalk, a city requirement. The Hilton Hotel Casino occupies the left side of the photo. Its life began in 1980 as Steve Wynn's Golden Nugget. Although it was more profitable than all the other early casinos combined, Wynn objected to the strict regulations imposed in New Jersey and sold it in 1986. It is still a remarkably successful casino, as well as a four-star resort.

INDEX